The Quest

Footsteps of Change

A Creation and Migration Story of the Indigenous People of North America

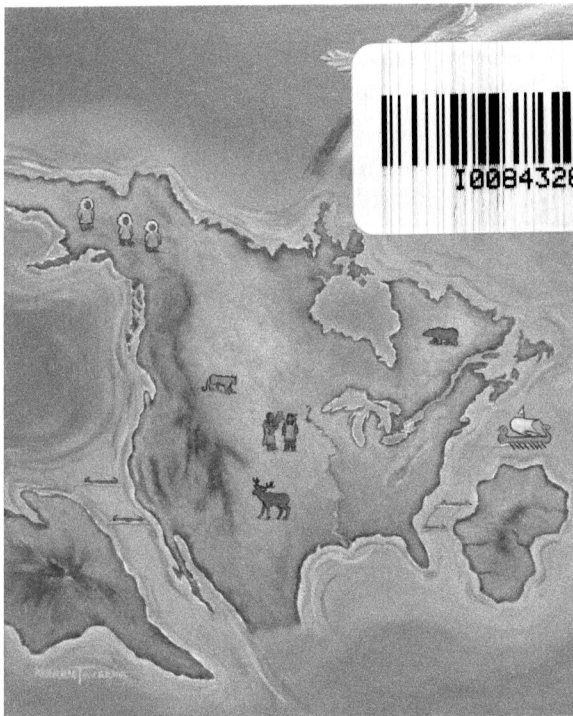

May your search for the good life lead you over
the red road of peace and happiness.

Donald L. Ensenbach

Book 5 of the *Whispers of the Past* Series

Other books by Donald L. Ensenbach
Kokopelli: Dream Catchers of an Ancient
Shadows Through a Spirit Window
Whispering Winds Remember
When the Spirits Move: A Native American Creation Story

STAIRWAY PRESS—APACHE JUNCTION

Front Cover Painting by Merrie Kapron Taverna
Cover Design by Guy D. Corp, www.GrafixCorp.com

STAIRWAY≡PRESS

www.StairwayPress.com
1000 West Apache Trail Suite 126
Apache Junction, AZ 85120 USA

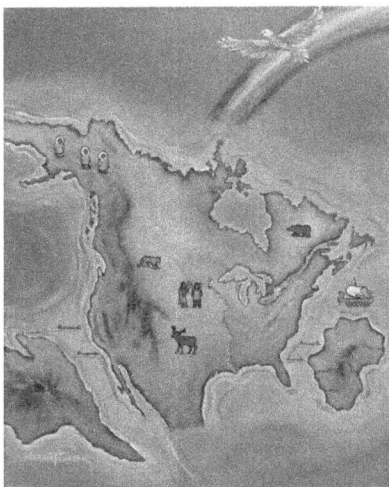

Introduction

LEGENDS AND MYTHS are the beginnings and beliefs of the Native American and indigenous people who have populated this continent since long before written languages were developed. Those of us who have interests in other cultures, realize that the oral telling of these stories are intended to teach as well as entertain the people to whom the stories are told. The Native American and indigenous people have cultural practices that only allow the storytellers to tell their stories during the winter season, as the other seasons are for planting, growing and reaping growing crops, or busily taking care of families, livestock, or mother earth, making jewelry, or weaving rugs. Of course, I am a bit facetious in using these illustrations rather than saying they go to work, school, or run businesses, just as all of us do to make our livings.

I would like to point out one thing you will find on all of the covers of my books. There is an eagle showing on each cover, and the reason is that the eagle is responsible for taking these people's prayers to the Great Spirit in the sky above. I find it interesting that we think of our God as living above us, as do these people. According to our beliefs, our prayers are directed to our God directly, whereas theirs are delivered to the Great Spirit by the high-flying eagle. Of course, most of the Native American and indigenous people have converted to the various faiths that they have been introduced to by our churches. I am hopeful that the legends and myths do not become forgotten as they turn away from their pasts, and think as most of us do, of the future.

It is always wise to remember, history is destined to repeat itself, and if that be the case, we must remember what has happened to our countries, culture, and our people when a decision is made that changes things. Please remember, although the red men owned NOTHING, they used EVERYTHING. UNTIL, the white man appeared, and slowly lost almost everything they valued, the land and their way of life.

Acknowledgements

ONCE AGAIN, I could not have possibly written this book without the approval and backing of my wonderful wife of almost 60 years, Opal. She even reminded me of the eagle to be placed on the cover of the book. I owe so very much to her as she stuck by my side through some hard times, and we have enjoyed, together, some very good and happy times. We take pride in our family of three adult children, who gave us five grandchildren, and they in turn have produced sixteen great-grandchildren (some through second marriages.) I can't thank all of them enough for all of the help and understanding they have offered to a man who doesn't pay as much attention to them as I should.

Next, I can't tell you how much I appreciate and respect the help my publisher, Ken Coffman, the owner of Stairway Press has given me. You probably won't believe this, but he delivers the orders of books I place through him right to my door. He has been a god-send to me and I want him to know that he is much appreciated.

The third, and a very important member of my team is Keith Ougden, my editor. He lives in Mesa during the winters, and he and his wife, Virginia spend the summers either at his home on the island of Cyprus or cruising the world on various cruise ships. He catches all of my errors, choice of words, punctuation, spelling, and typing. It is a Herculean task, but he endures my sometimes odd, and almost always, wrong opinions.

Thank you, Keith!

The last, and the most important person is the artist, Merrie Taverna, whose painting of the cover leads you the reader to buying my books. I can't tell you how important her pictures have become to me as each of the covers she has painted for me hang in our dining room, easily seen from the large living room.

Lastly, which should be first and foremost, I want to thank you, the buyers and readers of my books. Without you I would not be writing anymore at 81 years of age. The research is what keeps me going, but it is all of you that make it worthwhile. Thank you so much for helping to keep me alive and interested in writing these books. I hope to meet you sometime in the future, and hope that you will tell your friends and relatives about my books.

Watch for the next one which will be titled *Men of Metal and Crosses*. It will tell the story of the Spanish invasion of the Americas. I hope that book will be out sometime during 2021, if the Lord is willing, and everything goes as planned.

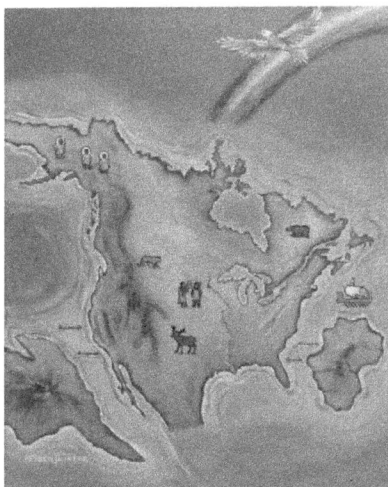

Prologue

THE YOUNG MAN, known as Running Deer, listened carefully to the words of his grandfather, Much-to-Know, chief of his tribe, as the old man taught the young man the knowledge of being a chief of his people.

"You must be fair and honest, believe in what you know to be true, be able to change your mind to another's idea if their chosen words convince you of their truth, be full of love and pride for our people, protective and understanding of their wants and needs. Be watchful and vigilant over the land that the Great Spirit has given us, and care for and honor it the best way you can. You will be a great chief if you learn the difference between right and wrong, but I see much danger ahead for you and our people. Watch closely for white men, riding on top of huge four-legged animals, carrying long weapons that spout much noise and kill animals and people when hit by their invisible arrows. They come to take what is ours and make it theirs. The animals we have been taking care of, the land that is our responsibility, and the very lives we have lived, will be taken from our people. Fear them as they will attempt to conquer us, and all things that we have known in the past or what we know now will become dust. You will see the ending of our tribe, or the beginning of a new tribe made up of them together with our people."

Not too many years after Running Deer and his grandfather,

Much-to-Know, had the above talk, white men approached the area in which he and his tribe lived. The white men sat astride huge animals they called horses, wearing shiny armor and holding metal shields that would deflect arrows, spears and knives. There were men on horseback, men walking behind in double file, all carrying long weapons, that when discharged caused very loud noises that frightened animals and people alike, and killed whatever the ball that emitted from the weapons hit. Yes, Running Deer saw these strange men approach from the south, and knew at that moment his, and his people's, world would change forever.

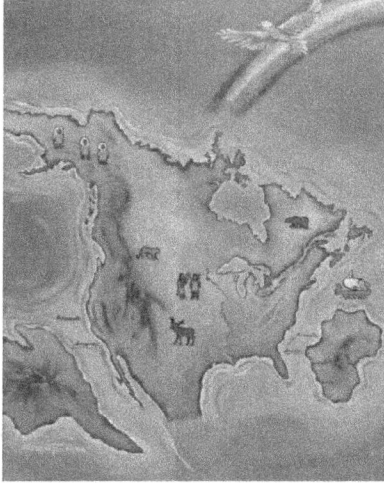

Chapter 1—The Beginning

IN THE BEGINNING, nothing but blackness existed, no earth, water, sky, moon, stars, or sun. From the blackness a bright shining disc appeared, one side white, the other yellow. Upon the disc sat a bearded man, the creator, the man who lives above. Rubbing his eyes as if waking from a sleep, he looked into the endless darkness. Wishing to see better, light appeared as if by his command. To the east streaks of dawn and to the west tints of many colors appeared.

Below him he saw a young girl sitting upon a large, soft cloud. Extending his hand to her, he asked for permission to join her. She asked, "Where have you come from?" He answered saying, "From the east where there is now light."

She motioned for him to sit beside her on the cloud, and they began to talk with each other. Asking what the "girl without parents" would like to have, together they wished for the sky to provide light and darkness during which they would be able to see during the day, and sleep at night. He began thinking and singing, "I am thinking, thinking, thinking, thinking," four times, for that is the magic number; "What can I create next?" And the sky appeared with

3

a shining sun entering from the east, many fluffy, white clouds, a moon and stars beginning to disappear in the east as the sun moved toward the sitting pair. The "girl without parents" spoke again asking, "Where is the earth upon which we might move, play, run, sit, walk, and work?" Waving his hands in a downward motion, the earth appeared and together they floated down from the cloud to rest upon the newly created earth.

With another wave of his hands, there appeared sun-god and small-boy, who became the third and fourth members of the group, whose various suggestions created the earth's great hills, mountains, prairies, and valleys with water surrounding the land. "This all looks beautiful, but how do we fill it with more beauty and life?" asked the "girl without parents." Small-boy asked "What about flowers, grasses, plants, trees, rocks and waterways to add to the beauty?" As if by magic, and the wave of the creator's hands, all of these suggestions began to exist.

Sun-god then suggested, "Human life is needed to take care of what you have created, such as animals, birds, fish, and people." The man who lives above asked, "What should these forms of life look like?" The "girl without parents" replied, "The animals should be formed to nurture the earth, ants and worms to live in the ground, fish and turtles to live in the water, bears, deer, and other animals to live on the earth, with birds flying through the air, and finally, people who have forms like small-boy and me to live on our mother earth and take care of her and her creatures. Each form of life should have a male and female form so they may multiply." As these thoughts were expressed, the forms of life appeared.

One last thought entered the creator's mind and he said, "We must offer the life forms methods of replacing those that have been all used up in their caring for mother earth. Four seasons will do nicely for the growing plants, trees, and human life. Human life will be produced in four colors, black, red, white and yellow. All living things will be expressed by their birth, learning, living to appreciate and enjoy their lives, and finally death to return to the earth to enrich it for their heirs."

Many other ideas were exchanged by the four participants, including fire, lightning, thunder, wind, ice, rain, snow, and the stages of the seasons. The ability for each of the creator's creations to change between the forms of creation (animals, birds, people, and vegetation could change to other animals, birds, plants, or people and back again as desired), and communication between all was allowed. Everything that we as people see or experience now was created at that time. The privilege of free will was important in the creation of the world in which we live; however that became a problem when each of the species—animals, birds, mineral, people and vegetation—began to change themselves often into another form of life and back again whenever they desired, creating confusion.

As the animals, birds, and people began living on the earth, some of the animals and birds became aggressive, attacking the people and other animals. Also, at that time, the four different colored people lived together. However, as time went on, adultery, arguments, envy, fights, and wars between the four peoples and animals disrupted life, and the four originals (creator, the "girl without parents", sun-god and small boy) decided to bring an end to the first world. Good people were sent underground to live with the ant people while the world's surface was swept away by fire, started when a meteor struck the earth near what is now known as the Gulf of California, killing the bad people and the huge animals and birds that threatened the people and each other.

A second world was created and a few changes were made to adapt to the desires and suggestions of the four original participants of creation. No longer were there animals who would harm people (dinosaurs and giant flying man-eating birds), and no changes between animals, birds, minerals, people, and plants were permitted. Laws of nature were given to animals, birds, minerals, plants, and trees, with only human people having free will. Also, the people were separated by color and given certain areas of the world within which to live. This worked well for a period of time, but once again, adultery, envy, fights, laziness, and wars bore witness to problems which needed fixing. The Ice Age ended the second world and sent the good people back under ground to learn togetherness and work ethics from the ant people that provided for the many living there.

A third world was formed from the remnants of the second, as the ice melted leaving the land and water much as it was before the ice froze the growing things. People returned by climbing the inside of a vine from the underground world into the bright new world with the hopes and dreams of bettering their lives through working together within separate areas, and with the people of their same color. This arrangement worked well for a while. How many years and generations is not known.

Once more, adultery, envy, fights, laziness, and wars became concerns to the four originals, who decided to flood the world with water, allowing the good people to return underground to learn from the ant families the important traits of living lives of ethics, togetherness, and working toward the betterment of all creation.

A fourth world, the world in which we now live, was offered to the people emerging into it by climbing the inside of a vine, with hopes that all creation would work together in peace and harmony.

Some red-skinned people emerged from the ground in the area we now call China, along with the yellow-skinned people. Each had traits not embraced by the other. The yellow-skinned people became adept at agricultural and art work, while the red-skinned people became hunters and gatherers. Both sought food and shelter, but the yellow-skinned people found growing foods from mother earth and building permanent homes near their food-growing areas served their needs best. The red-skinned people sought food from the animals and wild-growing plants and trees, following the animals as the animals moved northward looking for their foods. All people found eating raw foods was not good for them, and looked for ways to aid in their digesting the foods. A lightning bolt during a storm ignited a bush, and the people found that cooking foods over a fire improved the taste and digestive process. The only problem was that fire only occurred during lightning storms. How were they to get fire when there were no storms? During a dreamcatcher, a shaman of the red-skinned people asked the advice of a wise, old owl. "How can we get the fire we need to cook our meats and foods?" The owl answered, "By getting a lightning bolt from a storm, but I can't fly that high to get it for you. Why don't you ask a raven, which can fly much higher than me?" The shaman asked a white raven, and the raven consented to try to get the lightning bolt from the next storm. The white raven saw a storm cloud forming, then flew up as high as it could. When the lightning bolt jutted down from the cloud, it grabbed the bolt in its talons and flew down to the people with the bolt held close to its body. The bolt burned the raven's body, and that is why all ravens now have black bodies and wings. The bolt produced the first captured fire, which was then transferred to a small branch of a tree, which was carried, guarded, and relit on other branches by a young boy from each family, place to place, as they followed the food chain.

At first, men and women lived apart, each going their own way. Men did hunting, while women became gatherers. After watching the two groups for four moons, the creator decided to have the men walk over to the women's camp and introduce themselves to the women. As they arrived at the women's camp, the smell of the men, the way they looked, and their lack of manners turned the women away, demanding that the men leave the area. What good were these men to the women, anyway? So they were good hunters, ate better foods, were bigger and stronger, appeared to have something the women did not. Was that enough to invite them back? The creator had stopped, hiding behind a tree near the women's camp, and heard their complaints about the men. "They were untidy, they didn't bring us presents of food, they had no manners, appeared to be better at hunting, and just what was that thing they had that we don't?" Hurrying after the departing men, the creator began talking to them about bathing, shaving, bringing a present when visiting another's home, talking with respect to the people they met. This was a lesson for the men to learn, and since they had seen some of the women with whom they would have liked

7

to become familiar, they took the necessary steps to improve themselves. They began bathing in the river, shaved their faces, and found some fragrant flowers to rub over their bodies. Four days later, they picked some colorful and fragrant-smelling flowers; and taking those and some sweet venison meat with them, they returned, and were welcomed this time by the women at their camp.

As the men became familiar with the women, they each picked the one that they most wanted to impress and began to tell that woman about themselves. They saw the pretty teepee homes, smelled the freshness and sweetness of the flowers the women had brushed on themselves, and the men began to cook the venison meat they had brought. Since the women had not done any animal hunting, they let the men do the cooking. Some of the meat was not cooked thoroughly, at which time the women told them to cook it more. The women brought out some of the berries, mushrooms, nuts, seeds, and greens they had been collecting, and both men and women enjoyed the exchange of diets. This second meeting between the men and women had been quite successful, but the women wanted an opportunity to talk over the events as they had happened, unsure if they wanted the men to stay in their camp overnight. As the sun began sinking in the west, the men left the women's camp, walking back to their homes just four miles away.

After the men departed, the women had many comments about the protective way the men acted, how their deep-throated voices were like music to their ears, and they would certainly be good providers of food and other necessities. One of the women said, "The first time they came to our village they had not bathed, were dirty, unshaven, did not wear any clothes, did not bring us presents, and treated us badly. How and why is it they changed to the men who came to us today, completely different? We will wait a day, and then travel to their camp to see how they live." This was an acceptable idea, so the women made their plans to depart the day after the following day.

Meanwhile, on the way back, the men began talking about the

great homes the women had built, the way they dressed, looked and smelled, and how they would like being a provider for the women. The men also mentioned how they would enjoy living in a beautiful home like the women had, and wearing some of the clothes the women were wearing. As they approached their village, they laid down next to the trees they had used before as shelter, and fell asleep, snoring loudly. Their dream catchers were about the women they had met, the differences between them and the men. What was the meaning for the big orbs on their chests, and they didn't have anything dangling from between their legs?

The next morning, the men woke up as usual, readying themselves for the daily hunt, not bothering to wash or shave themselves, not wanting to take the time for finding lilac to rub on their bodies, not caring about the odor of their sweating bodies. They all went their own way in the hunt, but one man took a pathway leading back toward the women's camp. He stopped near the river where the women were washing their bodies and their clothes, still talking about the pleasant meeting with the men. One of the women said as he was listening, "These men seem to have caring hearts for everyone but themselves. We must teach them to become more attentive, enjoy the good things in life, and together we can create families that can follow us. My dream catcher showed me last night how they can help us become like 'the girl without parents', nurturing boys and girls, and all of us to become fathers and mothers like 'small boy' and 'the girl without parents'. Putting together the parts they have, with the parts we have will bring forth many children, who will help us occupy this earth. We will travel to their camp tomorrow and see how they live. If it is agreeable, we will begin to live together and produce many children."

The man who had overheard the conversation hurried back to his camp, calling all of the men together to tell them of the women's plan to visit them the following day. The men hurried about, placing tree limbs against the trees forming lean-tos, clearing the area of the scraps of food, garbage, and any other unsightly things. They dug a pit and buried the trash. They hung their weapons neatly on tree branches, shined their knives so they gleamed in the sunlight, gathered and knotted their hair in the back of their heads, and waited for the women to arrive. Yes, the second meeting of the men and women had been a success, but what was to follow?

As the women entered the area the men had considered their village, they brought with them some of the berries, mushrooms, nuts, seeds and greens they had collected for foods, offering them to the men as gifts. The men had saved some sika deer venison they had killed a few days earlier, and between the two diets, the men and women enjoyed a mid-day meal. After the meal was over, an extreme darkness occurred, as the moon blocked out the sun for a short period of time. The creator announced in a loud voice that was heard by all of the people, "The sun and moon are having relations which will birth a baby you will recognize as the man in the moon, and the moon will show its face each full moon for all time to be. This is a very pleasant event that both men and women will enjoy, and between the two of you, you will produce children that will fill the surface of mother earth. I have provided each of you the needs and the functions that will produce the children you will be responsible for." With that, the needs and functions of both the men and women became evident, were fulfilled, and the men and women began living together and became parents.

The creation of humans was not much different than that of the animals, birds, earth, sky, bushes, plants and trees, with the exception that everything other than what humans were given had natural boundaries and laws of nature to follow. But in the first world, animals, birds, people, plants and trees were given the opportunity to communicate between themselves and the people, and to become shape shifters, being able to change from what they were to another form of life. Humans were given free will, which made them the main care-takers of all of the birds, animals, fish, plants, and tree life on mother earth, using them as foods, clothing, or shelter as needed, or desired. During the second world, living things remained as they entered that world as birds, animals, fish, plant, or tree life, or humans.

This has been the creation story of the Apache Nation, the great N'dee, "the People."

Just as the Apache Nation has their creation story, the other groups of indigenous people have their own. The Eskimo and Inuit people of the Arctic area of Alaska, Canada and Greenland, say that the sky emitted water and ice that formed large oceans with pieces of land falling into the waters and, along with ice, formed islands. From the land, bushes, flowers, grasses and trees began to grow, and then animals and people began to appear. Fish, salmon, sharks, turtles, and whales, large and small, began to swim in the oceans, lakes, rivers and streams which flowed their way around and through the land, with great mountains rising, valleys falling, and beautiful ranges of prairies appearing. The great sun god appeared along with the moon and stars, although the sun only appeared brightly during the warm part of the year. The rest of the year was dark and bitterly cold. As the trees grew straight and tall, they were cut down and used for shelter and dugouts for kayaks and whaling boats. Those people crossed the Bering land bridge, and entered what is now called Alaska, having adapted to the cold climate while migrating from Asia, hunting and fishing as weather permitted, with gathering of edible foods mostly done during the short summer growing seasons.

The Navajo Nation explains their creation as their emerging from the first dark world by climbing the inside of a hollow reed planted in the ground of the first world by the sun god's child Begochiddy, up to a blue colored second world. They offended the Blue Swallow chief and were banished from that land. They returned to the hollow reed and resumed the climb on to a beautiful yellow third world. Upon reaching the third world, coyote, the mystical, mythical, good and bad character who presented itself as the people's helper, found a baby alongside one of the nearby rivers and took it to its home, hiding the baby from its father, the Water Monster. The Water Monster became angry and began to flood the earth. The people returned to the hollow reed and began climbing up to the fourth world, the world within which we now live. They emerged between six huge mountains inside what is now south-central China. They became nomads, searching for food, clothing and shelter, but found no place where they could settle down for more than short periods of time. Food sources were used up over time, and constantly moved on ahead of them. Sometime during their travels, they met with the Apache people and shared the Athabaskan language which both they, and the Paiute Nation, still speak in their reservations in Arizona and Oregon. They learned the Athabaskan language together in what is now known as Siberia. The Athabaskan language is only spoken along the coastlines of Siberia, the islands between Siberia and the coastlines of Alaska and Canada, the Paiute nation along the coastline of Oregon and the Apache and Navajo nations in Arizona. In fact, the Athabaskan language was the language spoken by the Navajo code talkers during World War II, which the Japanese military could not decipher. Although the Apache and Navajo people are considered cousins, there is not much love between them.

Other creation stories are told by the many indigenous peoples of the world. Almost all of them tell of advancing from a first dark world to successively brighter worlds until they reached the world in which they/we now live, usually the fourth world. The reasons for moving to another world are the firestorm as a meteor struck the planet killing off the dinosaurs and giant people, the ice age covering much of North America, and finally the flood, which is talked about in the Bible. Banishment from the first three worlds is usually attributed to greed, laziness, quarreling among themselves, wars, and committing adultery.

Another creation story involves a water bug diving through the water, bringing some mud from the bottom up to the creator, who rolled the mud into a ball. Rather than placing the ball into the water where it would sink, he saw a turtle swimming by and placed the rolled-up ball onto its back, saying, "I call you woo-tooie," which means in the Hopi language, "I call you mother earth." The creator rewarded the turtle for carrying mother earth on its back by awarding thirteen scales in the middle of its back shell, which represent the thirteen moon cycles that appear each year. That is how the Native Americans told time by the number of moons, and why many Native American/indigenous people say that we live on Turtle Island, North America. In fact, the Native American/indigenous people have stories they tell during the winter seasons about the different moons of the year, giving each of them names and duties they perform during each, as they travel from full moon to half, quarter, and baby moon lying on its back, before returning as the next full moon again. The moon became their calendar. The descriptions of the legends of the importance of the moon follow:

"Thirteen Moons on the Turtle's Back", taken in part from the book of the same name by Joseph Bruchac.

First moon is known as the moon of popping trees when the Frost Giant walks through the forest, striking the trees with his huge club and making the sound of trees cracking.

The second moon is known as the Baby Bear moon, because a young girl became lost in a snowstorm, and the family thought she was gone forever. But during the second moon she was brought back to her family by a mother bear. The girl told her family she had slept during the first moon with the bear family.

The third moon is known as the Maple Syrup moon as the maple syrup flows from maple trees during this moon.

The fourth moon is known as the Frog Moon, as the animals of the world took a vote as to how long winter would last. The moose said, as long as there are hairs on my body, beaver said as many as the scales on my tail, but the frog won out when he said as many moons as I have toes on my foot, of which there are five, giving us November through March.

The fifth moon is known as the budding moon, as at the beginning, winter did not want to leave, and the people went to the sun asking its help. The sun entered the home of winter and the walls of winter's home began to melt, forcing winter to move to the far north, and allowing buds to form on tree branches and flowers to sprout.

The sixth moon is called the Strawberry moon, as a young boy went walking alone into the woods near his village. He came upon two of the Little People, with whom he shared his meal. They took him to their home and taught him many important things, and sent him back to his village with strawberries. Those were the first strawberries the people had ever seen.

The seventh moon is known as the Acorn moon, as acorns begin to appear on the tree limbs, and the people begin to gather the acorns and save them for food during the winter, just as the squirrels do.

The eighth moon is known as the Wild Rice Moon. The bear and eagle saw the hunger the people were living through and asked the sun god to help the people find more food. The sun god looked down at the hungry people living near the shores of lakes and with an extra ray of sunshine, wild rice began growing, helping to feed the hungry people.

The ninth moon is called the Moose-Calling moon, as at that time of the year the moose becomes lonely and begins looking for a mate. The people call him from his home and direct him toward a future mate.

The tenth moon is called the Moon of Falling Leaves. The weather turns cooler, the leaves change to red or gold, and begin to fall from the trees when the wind blows.

The eleventh moon is called When the Deer Drop Their Horns, as it is time for them to gather together in their winter homes and begin growing new horns.

The twelfth moon is known as When Wolves Run Together. These animals howl louder when they assemble rather than being one lonely voice.

The thirteenth moon is the Big Moon, which completes the circle of the entire year. It is when the moons begin anew for the next year's cycle.

Arguments between animals occurred before man was created. After creating the animals and naming them, there were a few that didn't like the names they were given and complained to the Great

Spirit that they would like to change their names. The blue jay, coyote, and meadowlark complained, but the Great Spirit said, "No, I have given you names and those names will stay. This is my command, and that command is the law." Then, he told the animal world that He would not create man until the animal world would stop complaining. After hearing the words of the Great Spirit, the animal world became quiet, as he took away their rights to speak with one another. He allowed them sounds by which we identify them even now, such as the bleating of sheep, the caw of a crow, the scream of an eagle, or the hoot of an owl.

The legend of how man became the caretaker of all creation is all about a race around the Spearfish formation of red rock and sand that encircles the Black Hills of the Dakotas. The legend is told that all of creation, birds, animals, and man were equals. All lived in peace and harmony. Then, the animals, including man, decided on a race that would reward the winner with being the chief of all beings. As the race began, the deer jumped out and was way ahead. Seeing the great advantage he had, he laid down to rest. The buffalo took the lead with the turtle far behind. Man was near the middle when he saw a magpie that was happily flying above him. Man spoke to the magpie saying, "If you help me win, I will always take care of you." The magpie agreed, and flew up to where the buffalo was ahead. Landing on the buffalo's back, he rode that way until they approached the finish line, when it jumped off the buffalo's back and flew up ahead winning the race for man. Since that time, no man has knowingly ever eaten a magpie. Man was thus proclaimed chief of all the animals and birds. The race was so difficult that the runners' feet and hooves were rubbed raw, leaving a trail of blood around the Black Hills. That is why red earth covers the entire race track.

As you can see from the paragraphs above, there are many creation stories told by various indigenous people, but most have origins of emerging from the earth at various locations including the Grand Canyon of the Colorado River, the south-central part of China, the Pacific island of Mu, from the Atlantic island of Atlantis, and Scandinavia. There are other creation stories that speak of the people falling from a world above, or that the world is held up by strong leather ropes or cables anchored to the sky above. The use of telescopes allows us to look backward billions of years to find black holes which have such density that nothing can resist the pull of its gravity as the objects are pulled through it. We are learning more and more about the creation and movement of people over time through DNA and other technology. We may never know the complete story, but scientists are constantly probing the past looking for the trail leading backward to the beginning of time and the true story. It is certainly interesting to present the legends and myths of the many Native Americans and indigenous people who now live in North and South America. That is what I have attempted to do in my previous book, *When the Spirits Move* and this book, *The Quest: Footsteps of Change*. I am sorry for any duplications of stories, but I hope that you will find them still interesting and entertaining.

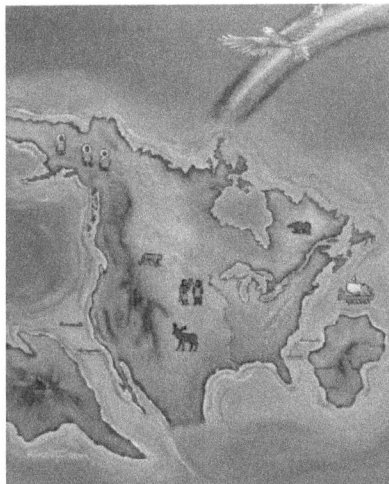

Chapter 2—Expansion and Migration

MOST ALL OF the various indigenous people have legends of the first world failing, and being set afire by the meteor that struck the Gulf of California, killing the large dinosaurs and giant people who were not helpful to creation. A second world replaced the first world, which brought forth many life style changes to all forms of life—animals, human and plant. Again, human forms were given the right to free will, and again the same problems developed as before. One difference in the second world was that the human race was given separate parts of the world within which to live. The black race supposedly emerged in Africa, the red race emerged from the salt mine in the Grand Canyon, the white race in Europe, and the yellow race in China. This second world existed for a longer period of time than did the first world, but once again, according to many people's beliefs, the Great Spirit saw fit to end this world by covering the earth with ice. This time period is considered to be about 25,000 years ago, and lasted for approximately 15,000 years.

17

This coincides with the time of the island of Atlantis being covered by rising Atlantic Ocean waters. There is also a legend of a Pacific island called MU, from which the Aztec people supposedly migrated by boats after the island continent was covered by water. What is hard to believe is that all of these events supposedly happened roughly about the same time that the ice melted after the indigenous people entered North America by walking across the Bering land bridge. Is it fact or fiction? Since neither you nor I were there, we cannot testify as to that part of history's authenticity.

The third world supposedly lasted longer than either the first or second world, but again there is the story, both in the Bible as well as the legends and myths of many Native American and indigenous people, that it ended with a great flood that covered all of earth's land. According to the pueblo people (Acoma, Hopi, Pima, and Tohono O'odham {Papago} people), the good people were allowed to enter the earth and live with the ant people to learn their ways of labor, endurance, collecting and the storing of foods and supplies for later use. After the earth was returned to livability, the people emerged from the earth and began living in the areas where they had lived before, except for some red-skinned people who emerged in south-central Asia. This was the fourth world, the world we now live in, according to many of the Native American and indigenous peoples of the Americas.

The last order of life was the creation of humans. There were black, red, white, and yellow people who were created by the Great Spirit and placed on the earth to care for the earth, animals, fish, and plant life, with the authorization to use each of them to feed, clothe and protect themselves from the elements as needed. The Great Spirit wanted and expected all of his creations to live and work together for the good of all; however, animal, human, and plant life did not act in their best interests much of the time. Anger, adultery, envy, gluttony, and stupidity were allowed to become a part of the human race through free will, and that became a large part of the downfall of all of us.

After man was created, there were many families that

separated and became known as clans. Their families followed animals, objects of nature, or symbols of courage, intelligence, strength or power, using their likenesses as the head of their clans. The Bear, Eagle, Parrot, Sun, Turtle, and Two-horned mountain goat clans are some of them. These clans followed directions their symbols suggested to them during their dreamcatchers, or other unworldly meetings they were believed to have experienced when using hallucinatory drugs, or starving themselves for vision quests. In most groups, the Bear clans were considered to be the leaders. One rule that all of the clans followed was that marriages were not to be allowed between members of the same clan. That is still a rule which is observed by nearly all Native or indigenous people, as that denotes a part of their own family.

A long time ago, before there were any colorful bushes, flowers, or trees, mother earth became distressed as she felt plain, ugly, and unappreciated. In her sighing, a small, little pink flower heard her, and said, "I will go out and add a pretty color to your robe that does not have any colors now." Mother earth cautioned the little pink flower that the wind demon would not like it, and would kill the little flower. But the little pink flower did grow and the wind demon did see it, and it did blow so hard that the flower was blown from the ground, and died. There were other flowers that tried to bring colors above mother earth, but each in turn died in the same way. Finally, a prairie rose said that it would try, and after growing to where it grew above mother earth's surface, and to where the wind demon could see it, the wind demon said, "Another flower to kill." As it got closer to the prairie rose, the wind demon inhaled the fragrance of the beautiful and sweet-smelling flower. The wind demon thought to itself, "Oh—how sweet! I cannot bring myself to blow out the life of such a beautiful flower with such a sweet breath. She must stay here with me. I must make my voice gentle, and I must sing sweet songs. I must not frighten her away with my awful noise." So wind demon changed, and became quieter. It sent gentle breezes, whispering and humming little songs of gladness over the prairies. Other flowers came up from the heart of mother earth, making her robe bright, colorful, and joyous. Even wind came to enjoy the beauty of the blossoms and the fragrances of the many colored flowers that decorated mother earth's apron.

Over time, the people of different colors, men, women, and families, decided to leave the areas in which their emergence had taken place. According to the Apache, Cree, Eskimo, Inuit, Navajo and other groups' history, their emergence place was located in what is now southcentral China. There were many more people who emerged from that area as well, red-skinned and yellow-skinned. The people of the yellow race increased their numbers quickly, and spread over large areas with expanding cultures of agriculture, architecture, art, ceramics, governmental structure, music and religion within what is now Asia. The increase in numbers meant that increases in food, clothing, and shelters were required, which necessitated the movement to areas in which each was more available. Planting and harvesting rice became the staple crop for the yellow race living in central Asia, primarily what is now China, and the people becoming known as Chinese.

Many, many centuries ago, as long as 50,000 years ago, a small family of people who were not of Chinese extraction were living in south-central China. Their red skin set them apart from the yellow-skinned Chinese people. How they arrived there, and from where, no one knew. They were not looked upon by the people of that area as being part of Chinese culture. They kept to themselves, and were never invited to participate in any of the economic, political or social events held by the yellow-skinned people who lived around them. Their way of life was predicated by the need for food, clothing and shelter, although no specific land on which to hunt or gather food was constantly available to them. If food was not available to them through hunting and gathering, they took food from the agricultural fields of the Chinese farmers, which caused the larger Chinese population to push the red-skinned people to the north and east of what is now known as China.

The red race was not quite as quick to expand, and were not accepted by the yellow race. They were not interested in settling down, but lived hand to mouth, being nomads, following the food chain wherever it led, walking through northeast China. The bears, birds, boars, caribou, deer, elk, mammoth, moose, sloth, and fish became the foods they sought, but when they came across agricultural fields, they fought for what they could take from the farmers, then were chased from that area to the next. Dogs were used to pull travois drags which carried most of their possessions, but the dogs were eaten when other foods were not available. They eventually came to a large mountain range stretching from west to east, and it had to be climbed and crossed. Yet, the people lived pretty good lives, starving one day, feasting the next. They ate foods that had been hunted and gathered, and other foods, only if it were growing wild or taken from people who had grown it. And normally, that is what they did, take it. Forever following the food chain as it moved northerly, then eastwardly, they came to the desolate plains northeast in what we now call Siberia. There was another animal that became available as a food source for these wanderers, reindeer. The ice, snow, winds, and bitterly cold weather did not deter the animals nor people, as both were following their necessary food chains. However, the foods from bushes, plants, and trees did not offer much to the people in the way of nutrition. Most of the time, those bushes, plants, and trees were stripped bare by the cold, snow, ice, and winds, or consumed by the animals ahead of them. The heavy skins of the animals the hunters killed for food became their bedding, clothing, head gear, footwear, blankets, or covering for their shelters, while the bones became frames for skis, sleds, and dwellings, or were used in tools, weapons, soups, or gnawing-foods for their dogs. Some of the skins were used to cover the shallow pit houses they dug into the snow. Still, the horrible gusty cold winds, the snowfalls, and the extremely low temperatures became their norm. Walking many hundreds of thousands of miles, through all kinds of weather, in some sunlight, but mostly darkness, guided by the starlit sky above and the tracks of the animals they followed, these people slowly, but surely, approached a broad roadway of ice leading east. The estimates of that pathway at the time were about six hundred miles wide, north to south and sixty miles long, west to east. It is now referred to as the Bering land bridge, which spanned the distance between Siberia and what is now Alaska during the ice age. That so-called land bridge separated what is now known as the Arctic Ocean from the Bering Sea.

On the way, the growing families split into many separate groups, all of whom continued to follow the food chain. To them, there was no spring, summer, fall, or winter. There was only the hunting season, all year round, and the prey was anything that could provide a meal, or more. This traveling took hundreds, even thousands of years, many thousands of miles, and many generations of these hardy people. The animals they followed were almost being herded, but always staying just far enough ahead of the hunters to keep their attention. Sometimes the animals would break through the ice and become stuck, so that the hunters would have easy killings, but it would be difficult to bring the dead animal up from where it had been stuck. Most often, some hunters would have to try to get ahead of the herd they were following, while the other hunters tried to encircle it. The surrounds became the most successful of hunting strategies for these nomadic people. Fish and sea life became foods these people became familiar with. When meat wasn't available, fish and sea life were killed by spears or harpoons. Seaweed was cut and eaten. Wooden spears were the first weapons the people made, with wooden handles and sharpened points becoming projectiles of death. Later, sinew was used to tie sharp stone points to the wooden shafts. Hatchets and knives with blades of bone or stone were carved or knapped, then set and tied into notched wooden handles for use in skinning animals, cutting meat from bone, or close-in fighting. In many of the battles conducted along the routes, men, women, and children of both sides were captured, and became slave labor, or even human sacrifices to the gods of their captors. The slaves were put to work working in the fields or homes of the Chinese captors, or carrying the items of the nomads, becoming scouts for them, as they walked their way toward they knew not where, but always following the food chain that moved ahead of them. The female slaves of the nomad people were used in many ways, setting up the camps, cooking, digging the pit houses, or whatever other work had to be done. By the way, the term cooking foods is used but warming foods would be more accurate, especially fish and meats, as it was very difficult to assure that the food was thoroughly cooked. Most of their foods were eaten raw or just browned. These people realized that following the food chain was their only hope of continuing to live, and that meant catching and killing their next meal. Because of the difficulties they lived through, they had great faith in their creator, "the man who lives above." It was he that provided the animals, fish, and all of the necessities of life. The sun, moon, stars, rain, bushes, plants, trees, snow, ice, and water covering the ground all came from the goodness of the creator.

The red-men's culture would not allow them to be enslaved, but when overcome by superior forces in battle, they succumbed rather than be killed. They, in turn, captured many people of the competing group and became slave holders as well. Many mixed-group children were born, lived and died. When forced to fight, the red men excelled at winning some battles, and when overwhelmed by numbers, tried to escape from those battles. They took what was needed for them to survive. Their complexions, physical makeup, and mental processes toughened as they walked their way through an ever-demanding landscape. They were always hunters and gatherers, never wanting to take the time and effort to plant or cultivate, never had patience to water, weed or harvest a crop of rice, or any other planted foods. These were primarily meat and fish eaters, with berries, leaves, mushrooms, nuts, and seeds furnishing the other foods that allowed them to simply live from hand-to-mouth, day-to-day. They followed the bears, birds, boar, deer, elk, mammoth, mice, moose, mountain goats, musk oxen, rabbits, sloths, wolves, and other smaller animals they could use as food that moved ahead of them.

Not all of the red race traveled together. As mentioned earlier, families split into groups called clans, following the animal or symbol representing their group. There were the bear, eagle, raven, spider, turtle, and wolf clans, and many other clans that developed their own identities which continue on to this day. Women followed their hunters, helping to butcher, clean, prepare for eating or packaging the animals the men had killed. Gathering foods other than the hunted animals was primarily done by the women of the clans. From within their bodies, hearts, and minds, they searched for their next meal and any comforts. Curiosity and hunger led them over the next hill to see what lay beyond, be it comfort, danger, excitement, food, mystery, or war. Furs of animals, bark and leaves from bushes and trees provided clothing and protection from the elements. Their homes were either hastily dug pit houses or teepees made of long branches tied together near the top, with the furs of animals stretched around the top smoke hole and around the outside of the structure allowing for protection from the cold, ice, rain, sleet, snow, and winds. Sleeping on furs provided little warmth, but it was better than sleeping on cold, icy ground. They learned how to start fires using sharpened wooden sticks put into shallow wooden crevices. They rolled the sticks between their hands to produce friction on the bottom of the wooden crevice. Small flames were caught by dried leaves and twigs, producing flame, gradually growing as larger dry branches were added. Then fire would be used in heating their foods, and warming their bodies. Also, drums, fires and smoke signals became a way of communicating between groups residing within hearing and sighting distances. Initially, men were responsible for shaping the wooden and stone tools for hunting, fishing, digging the pit houses, cutting the branches for erecting the teepees, and doing the weaving for clothing and blankets, with the women gathering and collecting the other foods and necessities of life, cleaning and cooking, besides delivering children.

After arriving at different places throughout their migration, groups of people began to stop along the way and build small family villages. Near the east end of the Bering Land Bridge a group of people chose to leave the wandering to the larger group, establishing villages in the area now known as Alaska. That first groups were comprised of members of the Raven, Wolf and Eagle clans, which became the Tlingit culture. Their creation story is different than the one of the Apache or Navajo Nations. Their legend is that their forefathers were terrified by ghosts and took refuge in a very large clam shell. The clam shell rested on a beach along what we now call the Pacific Ocean. A white raven heard them talking inside the clam shell and flew down next to the shell, then broke it open. The people emerged and began looking around them. They had emerged at a time when shadows were the only things they saw, for there was no sun, moon or stars. They asked the raven if it could provide them with more light. The raven told them that the grandfather who lived above them kept the light in a large wooden box in his home. The Tlingit people asked the raven to get the grandfather to release the light, but the raven said the grandfather would not relinquish the light easily, but it would try. The raven picked one of the Tlingit women to become pregnant, with the raven becoming the human baby. After birth, the grandfather took the woman and baby boy into his home above. As the baby grew, he planned to wait for the grandfather to leave the home for a short while, and during the grandfather's absence, the baby would open the box, release the sun, moon and stars, and escape with them through the smoke hole in the grandfather's home. The boy carried out his plan, taking the contents of the box in his hands, then changed himself back into the raven. Clutching the heavenly bodies in its claws the raven flew up to the smoke hole but got stuck trying to fly out. Unfortunately, the smoke hole was smaller around than the raven, and when the grandfather returned and saw what the raven had done, he lit a fire under the raven's body. The white raven became blackened, but did squeeze through the hole to escape, placing the sun, moon and stars into the sky as you see them today. That is the reason all ravens are now black. Returning to the Tlingit people, the raven told them it would shield them from ghosts, and that they would live forever. Of course, that was not to be. Upon seeing the heavenly bodies of the sun, moon, and stars in the skies above them, the Tlingit people built their long multi-family homes from the tall cedar trees that grew along the areas in which they chose to live and forged a very good life for themselves and their families, extending even to now. They chose to live near the coastline of the great ocean, so that they could both hunt game animals inland and fish for food from the waters. Many totem poles were carved and set-up to honor the raven, bears, and eagle, which represent great intelligence, strength and family values.

The Tlingits, along with other peoples of the northwest coast, believe that the salmon is a race of immortal men who lived beneath the sea during the winter, and in the late spring, assume the form of salmon, swarming up the rivers in huge numbers to offer themselves to humans as food. But this self-sacrifice did not destroy the salmon-men. The fishermen stripped the flesh from the fish and returned the bones to the waters from which they took the fish. The bones would be reborn as men, who would return to their undersea home for the winter, and return as salmon again the following spring.

A second family group of these people is known as the Haida Nation, and live north in the Yukon Territory. They live, much as the Tlingit people, near the coastline of the Bering Sea and the Gulf of Alaska extending down from the Yukon Territory toward what is now known as the Kenai Peninsula. Their long and narrow multi-generational wooden homes were also built with cedar planks cut from the tall cedar trees that grew in the area. Both the Haida and Tlingit people became great fishermen, outstanding carpenters and traders, who would seek whales for food and oil, and used whale bones for many building materials, tools and weapons. The huge cedar forests provided the wood to build the large multi-family long houses and multi-person whaling vessels, which could take years to construct from start to finish. Smaller canoes were carved from the wood and used for fishing for salmon. Salmon fishing provided, and still provides, a huge part of their diet and lives. Netting, spear fishing, and setting traps to which the salmon are, and were, lured are used in their fishing tactics. A good salmon fishing season of four months would store enough salmon for a full year. Totem poles signifying accomplishments or honors for families, individuals, or villages were carved from the tall, straight cedar trees. The tops of the totem poles were carved to represent the animals, birds or fish that were considered to be protectors of the people who carved them. All types of bowls, cups, pots, skis, sleds, snowshoes, toboggans, tools, utensils, and even large multi-family warehouses were formed from the trees, with the bark being used in weaving blankets, clothing, footwear, and as roofing and insulating materials.

Raven was not recognized as the creator, but was of the creator. It became a symbol of good, and bad, as the raven had two sides to its spirit. The raven was no ordinary bird. It had remarkable powers and could change itself into whatever form it wished. It could change from a bird into a man, and could not only fly and walk, it could swim underwater as fast as any fish. The Tlingit people tell of a time that the raven turned itself into an old bearded man walking along the trail through a forest. He became aware of being hungry, and saw a lake in which the Tlingit men were fishing. The raven dove into the water and began taking the bait from the hooks, then giving a little tug of the line. The men began to pull up the string on which the hook and bait had been attached, but found no bait nor fish on any of the hooks. One of the fishermen pulled up his line just as the old man (raven) was taking a bite of the bait. The hook snared the lower jaw of the old man, which the old man quickly detached from its face as the fisherman pulled it to shore. The appearance of the lower jaw and the long beard frightened all of the men, who ran back inside the home of their chief. Raven, still in the form of the old man, covered himself with a long blanket, hiding his face from the crowd. As the jaw and beard was passed around to the men within the circle, the raven, still in the old man's form, picked up the bearded jaw, and before anyone could see what had happened, replaced it on its face. Turning back into a bird, it flew out of the smoke hole in the top of the roof and disappeared. So, raven was known as a benefactor as well as a trickster.

Giants were another nemesis for the Tlingit people. There was one giant that would come into their villages, grab some people and take them to his home, where it would fry them, then eat them. This happened quite often, and at a meeting of the residents at one of the villages, a brave man of that village said he was going to kill the giant. The next day, he went and laid down in the middle of the path from where the giant came, and played dead. The giant came on the path, and seeing the man lying down, looking dead, said, "Here is a human that I will not have to kill. He makes it so easy for me. I will take this man back to my home and eat him. He is still warm, but I will cook him in my fire before I eat him." It carried the man to its home, dropping him in the middle of the floor, and left to go outside to fetch some wood for the fire. The giant's son came into the home, but the man caught the son and with a knife held to the son's throat asked, "Where is your father's heart?" The son was very scared and said, "His heart is in the left heel." The man hid next to the doorway waiting for the giant to return. As the giant returned to the house, his left heel entered the home first, and the man plunged the knife into it. The giant was killed instantly, but began to speak. "Though you killed me, I will continue eating you humans forever." The man said, "No you won't as I will cut you into little pieces, and you will never bother us again." As he was dissecting the giant, the little pieces began to fly around, biting the man, and that is how mosquitos came to be.

Another group of wanderers crossed the Bering land bridge much later, following the food chain to the north. These people also decided to remain in the cold arctic air, and started villages. They became known as Aleut-Eskimos, people who reside along the coastlines of Alaska and Eastern Siberia. Many of those people made it across the Bering land bridge before it became submerged, while others remained in Siberia. Some of the people became stranded on islands that remained above the waterline as the land bridge became submerged.

One of those islands was where a young boy lived alone for a long time. He was fond of picking up rocks just for exercise. As he grew older, the rocks he picked up got to be bigger and heavier all the time, and his strength grew. Eventually, he decided to go to another island and find a mate. He carved out and paddled a small canoe to the nearest island, and began walking inland. He came to a village, and saw a light inside the doorway of a home and peered in. He saw a beautiful young woman inside combing her long black hair with the bones of salmon. He called into her, and she invited him into the home and fed him some heated salmon. When the men of the village heard that a stranger had entered their village and was being entertained by one of their most eligible and sought-after young women, a challenge was made for a contest between the champion of the village and the visitor. The challenge was a canoe race around a nearby island, and the winner would win the right to kill the loser. As the two competitors pushed off, they were side by side, but as the race went around the island, the local racer went into a sizeable lead. The visitor's canoe was covered by a beluga whale's skin, and he asked the canoe to turn into a beluga whale and swim underwater to pass the other canoe. At the end of the race, the visitor had won, and killed the local man, putting a spear through his body. The village considered the local man to be a very valuable resident, and tried to remove the spear from his body, but could not. They asked the visitor to remove it and after he did that, the local man came back to life, and the two men became great friends.

There was a great bear hunter who lived in the village of the Aleuts, who was successful every time he went bear hunting. He had killed so many bears that he was considered the best bear hunter who had ever lived. A bear hunter from another village came to ask his help in finding and killing a bear with a white face and four white paws. That bear lived in a forest near the other hunter's village. The great bear hunter agreed to go with him to find and kill the bear as it had become a killer of the bear hunters who had tried to hunt it. The great bear hunter went into the forest looking for the bear with the white face and four white paws. He came face-to-face with that bear, and before he could raise his bow and nock his arrow, the bear spoke to him. "I know that you are a great bear hunter. You have killed many of my family, but I too was once a great bear hunter, and so successful that the other hunters in my village became jealous. They went to our shaman and asked how they could rid themselves and the village of me. The shaman had them lay a bearskin of a bear I had killed seven days before as my pillow, and then he changed me into this bear you see before you today. I will take pity on you today, but I urge you to never hunt for bears again. If you do hunt us again, I will tear you apart. Will you do that for me?" The great bear hunter was ashamed of himself for having killed so many bears, and agreed to the request. He went back to his village, and began hunting rabbits. The change was noted by other hunters in his village, and near the end of the fall season, before the bears go to hibernate, they asked him to accompany them one more time to hunt the bears. He turned them down several times, but finally agreed to go with them after putting on a disguise. Since the other hunters were not as adept at finding where bears would be at this time of the year, he found himself alone nearing the forest. The white faced and white pawed bear came out toward him, ready to tear him apart. He pleaded with the bear for one more chance to return home to see his mate before being torn apart. The bear agreed, but with the stipulation that the hunter provide the bear an opportunity to meet the shaman who had initiated his change from a man to a bear. The man agreed and they went into the village, and the man took the white-faced bear to the home of the shaman. The shaman's home was closed, but the bear tore open the door and walked in on all four feet, confronting the shaman. He demanded, "Return me to the man I was before you put this curse on me, or I will tear you apart." The shaman asked the bear to lay down in his home, and the shaman began stripping the bear fur from its back, and the rest of its body. By morning the man had been freed of the bearskin, and became a human again. It is said that he, nor the other hunter, ever hunted bears again.

Snowshoes, skis, and dog sleds are used extensively in the Yukon, Alaska and northern Canada when one is required to go from place to place during the winter snows. In fact, even now there is an annual very long dog sled race over 8-15 days and over 938 miles. The race is called the Iditarod, which is one of the premier races in all of the Americas that takes place entirely in Alaska. The dogs are trained by the musher, who is the man who rides the back of the sled pulled by a minimum of five dogs, but the musher usually trains 15 dogs, using most of them during the long race, roughly encouraging the dogs to run along the route from Anchorage to Nome, Alaska. It takes a lot of courage, determination, and stamina to complete the race for dogs and musher. The winner is touted by the residents of Alaska during the entire year following his victory, but at the start of the next race, all is forgotten, and the many hopeful contestants start all over again.

The summers in Alaska are much warmer and easier for the people to endure, however it is said that the mosquitos are so very large and hungry, that they (laughingly) can carry a person off with them. Hunting and fishing are still carried out throughout Alaska, Canada and the Yukon areas, and there is oil withdrawn from areas there, primarily from the great Prudhoe Bay. In fact, the state of Alaska pays its inhabitants a royalty check for each man, woman, and child annually from the taxes paid to the state by the oil companies.

The people I have told you about are the people who remained near the Bering land bridge. Many of their children's descendants still live there. These people honor their gods, histories, symbols of power, and other important things, by constructing huge totem poles displaying carvings of the raven, bear, fish, and other symbols of their history. The totem poles are carefully carved from the tall, straight cedar trees found in the area; a tree is felled and stripped of its bark, then carved. Most times, the eagle, raven or bear, as symbols of courage, cunning and strength, are at the very top of the carved pole, which is then painted in colors that best represent the object or event of which it is supposed to remind them. The poles are never touched or repaired as they deteriorate in the extreme weather that country is known for. If another object or event becomes more important, another totem pole is carved and erected in front of the older totem pole by the family or village it represents. The totem pole and its meaning is a very sacred object for the home or village it stands before. The residents can look back in time, see and remember the important objects and events that formed their prior cultural history.

Igloos, or houses made with blocks of ice, were used as homes by the Aleut Eskimos until wooden buildings were erected as permanent homes. Shielding the people from the snow, ice storms, and bitter winds was all that stood between the people and certain death from freezing and starvation. The ice was also used as water when thawed, which helped to keep them alive. The skins of animals laid on the top of the ice inside the homes were of slight help in trying to keep bodies warm while sleeping.

The first people to cross the Bering land bridge were the Apache and Cree people. They followed the food chain as it led east and south, across and down through what is now Canada and into the United States. The brooks, creeks, lakes, and streams offered water abundantly, which also attracted the animals they sought for food—the bear, deer, elk, and mountain goats led them to the turkeys, and other smaller, but edible, animals located in the forests of both lands. Since these people were primarily meat eaters, the animals they encountered were most often hunted and killed near the places at which they watered. Because of the warnings originally given by the Great Spirit to the first people, only what was needed for food, clothing, and shelter were killed or used by the people. Preserving life was considered as both practical and necessary for their future wellbeing. Realizing there were four seasons—spring, summer, fall and winter—for the birth, growing, living, and death for all of nature, the people organized their hunting accordingly, seeking out the animals that provided meat, and bones for soup, tools, and weapons. The hides and pelts for clothing, bandages, bedding, and wrappings for shelter were collected. Nothing was discarded that could be put to use. An area for refuse was always designated around the village in which they lived, generally downwind of it. Sometimes it was a dugout pit, other times at the bottom of a ridge outside the village. The areas along the waterways were kept clean alongside the villages where water for drinking and cooking was drawn. Bathing, washing dirty clothing, dishes, and pots were done downstream.

The Apache, Cree and Navajo people were the first to move east and then south after entering North America, and proceeded across the receding ice-covered land. The Apache band began drifting southward into what is now the Northern United States, while the Cree remained near the lower central part of what is now Canada. Some of the Apache people left the larger group and walked to the west, coming to the Pacific Ocean area of what is now Oregon. They became the Paiute Nation, who live there still, and some still speak the Athabaskan language they learned in Siberia.

It is hard to imagine sleeping inside a shelter, with ice as its flooring, even after using hides and fur as bedding. The warming of the planet was helpful to the animals and these people seeking the light and warmth while following the food chain, however it had its consequences as well. The ice melting at the north and south poles affect the balance of the world and the weather changes we all have seen occur. Rain and snow storms affect water levels, as does the sunlight affect evaporation. But for now, let us go back in time and travel with the various Native American/indigenous people to the places each of them selected for their homes.

The Salish people also migrated across the land bridge into North America. A legend about the Salish people, also known as Flatheads because of the way they wore their hair flattened toward the front, is that they honored the creator, the old man in the sky, and recognized the symbol of a coyote as being good, but considered the mountain sheep as bad medicine, or evil. There was a time long, long ago that the coyote went up to the upper world crying profusely. The old man in the sky asked the coyote why it was crying, and told it that if it didn't stop crying its tears would flood the land. The coyote told the old man in the sky, "I have no one to talk with in the world down below, and I get very lonely. I would like people to talk with and whom I could care for." The old man in the sky said, "Then stop this shedding of water. If you will stop annoying me with your frequent visits, I will make people for you. Take this rawhide bag and go up to the place where you can find red mud, gather some together in this bag, and bring it back to me." The coyote did as it was told, gathering the bag full of red mud, and began walking back to the hole leading to the upper world. It became tired along the way and laid down to rest for just a short time. It fell asleep, and during that time a mountain sheep ram came across the coyote and the bag of red mud. It thought it would play a trick on the coyote and snatched from the paws of the coyote the rawhide bag containing the red mud. He dumped the bag of red mud out on the ground, filled the bottom half with black, white, and yellow mud and the top with the red mud, and then replaced the bag in the paws of the sleeping coyote. Soon the coyote awoke and resumed walking toward the hole in the sky leading to the upper world. Arriving at the hole it began walking up the stairs toward the home of the old man in the sky, and after knocking on the door, entered the home and handed the bag to the creator. Inside the home the light was not too bright, and as the old man in the sky began to take the mud from within the bag and make figures of men and women, he had unknowingly withdrawn all of the red mud off the top and gotten to the black, white and yellow mud in the bottom part of the bag. That is why we have black, red, white and yellow skinned people on this earth. The Salish now reside in Oregon.

Many other clans began walking across what is now Canada, stopping along the way, setting up camps from where they hunted and gathered. The largest contingent of them were called the Cree, and they are still the largest group of all of the indigenous people in Canada. As stated before, they settled along the border of Canada and the United States. There are two basic tribes of Cree, the woodland and prairie tribes. Since there is much of both— woodland and prairie—on both sides of the border, the Cree live on large swaths in the southcentral part of Canada and the northcentral part of the United States. They lived around the Great Lakes of North America, and were great hunters and gatherers. Their hunters provided mostly deer and moose, but when those were not available, they ate fish from the lakes and gathered wild rice from the wet areas around the lakes. The women did most of the work, gathering the foods other than the meat and fish, cleaning and cooking and having children. They were agriculturists, not warriors, unless forced to fight.

The creation story for the Cree Nation is next. According to their myth, a man and woman looked down from a stark world above and saw the greenery offered by a plush world below. Seeing a spider web that stretched from their world down to the world below, they began climbing down. They had been warned by the Great Spirit not to look down as they climbed down the web, but they did look down and began falling, landing in a giant eagle's nest. A bear and wolverine, which had seen their fall, climbed up the rocky bluff and rescued them before the eagle returned. The bear took it upon itself to teach the two people how to live on the earth—places to seek shelter from the weather, how to gather foods from plants and trees, how to hunt animals for food and clothing, and the careful use of fire. The bear warned them to kill animals only for food or protecting themselves, and not to waste any of the items the Great Spirit provided for them. They began to explore the world they had fallen into, traveling north, south, east, and west, but settling near the place of the eagle's nest in south central Canada.

Ayas was a handsome young Cree man, whose father had been killed by a monster from the great lake near where his family lived. His mother had married another man from the village, who had been an abuser of his mother. When Ayas had told other clan members about the abuse, the stepfather had taken Ayas with him on a hunt that took them to a deserted island where other monsters lived, and then left him there. Ayas lived in a small grass hut he erected for himself, from which he hunted and gathered food for himself every day. He met a monster from the water that surrounded the island where he lived, and they began to battle. Ayas first used his bow and arrows to try to kill the monster, but the monster ducked all of the arrows being loosed toward him, and advanced toward Ayas. Ayas used a spear that he had brought with him, throwing it at the monster, but once again the monster ducked the thrown spear. Ayas pulled out his skinning knife as the monster approached and started jabbing and ripping the monster in the chest and down toward its big belly. As the knife cut into the belly, some people jumped out of the belly and ran behind Ayas. The monster finally died and there were twenty-one people who were released from the monster's big belly, and they proclaimed Ayas as their chief of the village island near the present location of Montreal.

Returning to the Apache and Navajo people, they continued to follow the food chain east eventually reaching the Canadian Rocky Mountains. As they saw the great heights and the difficulty of the climb, they decided to turn southward, following the western edge of the mountains, following the great herds of buffalos, deer, and elk. Finding warmer weather as they expanded to the south, the Apache and Navajo people entered what is now the northern states of Idaho and Montana of the United States of America. The land was teeming with buffalos, deer, and elk in the valleys and big horned mountain goats in the hills and mountains. Those four animals became the source of most of their meals, as they followed the herds southward. The buffalos had very poor vision, and as they were always grazing for food, never saw the hunters surround the herd, or stampede them toward cliffs from which they fell and were killed. The women did most of the butchering, saving all they could get for food. They stripped the hides for clothing and covering the exterior of the teepees, while the men used the bones for tools, utilities, and weapons. As the herds moved south and eastward, the Apache and Navajo clans followed closely behind. As they killed the buffalo, the butchering was done near the spot on which they were killed, and nothing other than the head and skull was left behind. The skulls of the buffalo were not saved as they were heavy, hard to carry, and had nothing of value other than for soup bones. There were said to be millions of buffalos throughout the United States until overkill took place between the 1850's to the 1870's, when the herds faced near extinction. As the railroads were built, those companies hired hunters to kill the buffalos as they hindered the laying of tracks by getting in the way of the workers, and caused many costly wrecks when the trains hit the huge animals. They became over-hunted by the many people, Native Americans, indigenous, and white hunters, and faced near extinction. The railroads employed hunters such as "Buffalo Bill" Cody to rid the areas around the route of the train tracks of the "dangerous and costly" buffalos. It has been just recently that the buffalo herds are increasing in the many National Parks, museums, zoos, and individual farms and ranches across the United States and Canada.

Illness followed these nomads, and they sought ways to heal through all types of methods. Many people were dying as the travelers stopped along the way. There was one rock formation that stood out in the area at which they had stopped, and it was called "wishing stone." One evening during the medicine man's dream catcher, the "Great Spirit" came to him and said, "Tell your people I will send a messenger to them. On the day after the moon is full, gather all the people next to the wishing stone. Tell them to bring all of the sick ones." The medicine man told the members of the clans the words of the Great Spirit, and they all gathered near the wishing stone on the designated day. All were dressed in their finest garments and the sick were all with them. As the sun reached its peak, the medicine man pointed toward the tallest peak where they all saw the vision of a beautiful young woman. She floated down to the wishing rock, where she sat, resting. She said, "Great Spirit above has heard your prayers and has sent me to help you. Come near to be healed of your sicknesses." The people crowded near her, touched her, and soon were well. She resumed speaking saying, "I will come again some time. But you must do what I tell you to do. You must plant these seeds I give you. It is camas seed, and in springtime it will have blue flowers. There will be so many flowers it will look like a blue lake. In the fall, gather the roots and eat the roots. If you do this the sicknesses will not return." Then she disappeared. The roots were taken along wherever they moved, and planted each spring. The camas plant is native to Canada and the United States, growing wild primarily on the prairies, and gardens wherever planted. Camas is part of the lily flower family.

Of course, as the clans moved, they encountered clans of other groups. These clans were the pueblo people who were written about in my previous book, "When the Spirits Move." This led to much bloodshed as those people who had hunted and gathered in those areas for hundreds of years felt that the invaders had no business entering their areas. Sometimes the pueblo people, Hopi, Acoma, Zuni, Pima, and Tohono O'odham, etc. would plant their corn, squash, beans, melons, and other crops, then leave the area for hunting and gathering expeditions. While they were gone, the Apache and Navajo groups would come into the planted areas and steal the products that had been growing. When the pueblo people returned, they found that their crops had been stolen, and that what remained had been destroyed by the invaders who were long gone by then. It was times such as these that made it necessary to search for other foods, such as birds, coyotes, dogs, rabbits, squirrels, mice, and even worms, just to survive the cold, long winters. According to one legend, when the clan returned to find their crops stolen, the chief prayed to the Great Spirit, asking for help in feeding his people. The Great Spirit sent a sign through the chief's dream catcher to replant the crop of corn, squash, and beans immediately, and within two months the corn, squash, and bean fields grew and could be harvested. Thus we hear the term "Indian Summer."

Another legend is of the clan which returned from their hunting trip to find their crops completely destroyed, so they sent their hunters out to find and bring in some rabbits for future meals. The hunters all left, but there was a young, unmarried woman who had been watching over her elderly mother and father rather than marrying. She decided to search for rabbits too. Her mother, father and she had been eating the leftovers and items that the other members of the tribe threw out. As she searched farther and farther from their camp, she began finding and killing more than her share of the rabbits. After a while, she felt that darkness was overtaking her, and she had lost her way, and knew not in which direction her camp was located. She spotted a small cave with a very narrow opening in the side of a hill and climbed in. After skinning one of the rabbits and starting a fire she began to fry one of the rabbits for her dinner. The aroma of the cooking meat drifted out of the cave and was carried by the night air to a prowling, hungry giant coyote. It approached the opening of the cave, asking for a piece of meat to eat. Realizing that it was a hungry coyote that meant her no good, she threw out one of the rabbit's legs, hoping to satisfy the animal. But no, the animal demanded more.

After she had given all of the rabbits she had caught, with nothing more to give, she told the coyote she only had the clothes on her back left. Two spirits heard her pleas and came to her rescue, killing the coyote, and bringing her a large number of rabbits. Then, in the morning, they showed her the way back to her camp and left her. She walked into the camp with the string of rabbits on a pole and the hunters began praising her on her skill for hunting. That evening, one of the young hunters came to the teepee in which she and her parents lived and asked her to marry him. He promised to hunt and care for all of them for as long as he lived. Chivalry lived long before it became fashionable in Europe.

Weather was so very important to the people. Music, chanting, drum beats, flutes, and dancing were, and are, petitions to the "Great Spirit" to bless the earth and its people with items they want or need. Also, rain dances are very important; they ask for moisture, rain or snow, in moderation. The Hopi rattlesnake dance is actually a prayer for rain, and is one of the most sacred prayers in the world. The chanting of the crowd, drum beats, flute music and the movement of the dancers with the rattlesnakes held cross ways in their mouths are appeals for the much-needed rains to ripen the crops in the fields. Following the ceremony, the snakes are released to deliver the prayers to the "Great Spirit" in hopes of the blessing of rain to fall on the people's crops. Actually, this ceremony was presented to President Theodore Roosevelt in Walpi, Arizona in 1913, and the Congress of the United States in Washington, DC in 1923 in front of the steps of the Capitol building. The following day supposedly there was a hard rainfall around the area. The legend, or myth, that tells the story on how the dance was found involves a young boy named Tiyo, who lived with his family of the Snake clan next to the great Colorado River within the bowels of the Grand Canyon. His curiosity of where the river went after flowing by the village led him to ask his father, the chief of his tribe. His father answered that he did not know, so Tiyo made a promise to his family and himself that he would discover the river's destiny while on his quest to find out what he was to become in adult life. He built a canoe, and upon the day he was to begin his search for his future, his parents gave him prayer sticks before he climbed into the canoe and let it drift for many days before bumping into an island.

Climbing out of the canoe he saw a small home nearby, asked for permission to enter, and entered it upon receiving the invitation. It was the home of spider woman, who was given some prayer sticks, then fed Tiyo, and asked him what he wanted, and where he was going. After telling her of his quest, spider woman led him to several sacred and secret places, but lastly took him to a cave in which the sacred snake clan members sat in a circle as men would do. After giving the council members some prayer sticks, he began asking questions. After a while with his questions and their answers, the men decided to allow him to see their two daughters and offered him his choice for one to be his wife. He chose the most beautiful and the two were married by the chief of the clan. The snake-men were the ones who taught him the music and motions to do the rattlesnake dance in appealing for moisture, and he took his wife back to the clan from which he had originally come. He taught his clan members the dance and they have performed it from that time to now in asking for rains for their fields. Tiyo also became the chief of his tribe after his father died.

Animals and plants were very important to all people, whether they were Native Americans or those who came from elsewhere. Since both had been created before people, the Great Spirit told the animals and plants to remain awake for seven days and seven nights. Of the animals, only the mountain lion, owl, and panther remained awake for all that time, and because of that, they are the only animals that see in the dark. Among the trees and other plants, the cedar, pine, holly, and laurel were the only ones to remain awake over the seven days and seven nights. The Great Spirit told them, "Because you watched and kept awake as you had been told, you will not lose your hair in the winter." So these trees and plants retain their greenery all year around.

Plants that produce colorful flowers, or trees that produce leaves, do so at specific times of their life cycle. All living things have a life cycle, a birth, living time, and death. Our red-skinned brothers and sisters believe they will return to life in a different form after their death, and I have not heard of anyone denying that they have slight remembrances of similar circumstances they recognize as having lived through, perhaps in a prior life. Heaven and the "happy hunting grounds" represent the same places to the Native Americans, indigenous people, Christians, or Muslims, but according to some people, sometimes it takes more than one lifetime to earn that place. A second life as a person or animal, or a purgatory, may give us another opportunity to earn that sacred place. I know of no one who wants to hurry that trip along, do you?

The Paiute people entered North America by way of the Bering land bridge and some followed the Pacific Ocean coastline southward, and those people stopped in Oregon. Their Athabascan language was learned in Siberia, and is the same as the Apache and Navajo language used on their reservations in Arizona. Although the Paiute people were hunters and gatherers, their hunting methods were not up to the standards of other nomads. That is why they were not a very wealthy tribe, wearing few leather clothes, owning few items of worth, intent to live on less, living a peaceful lifestyle. Fishing and agriculture were their main occupations along the coastline, although the group split up and some of their people live in California, Idaho, Nevada, Utah and Arizona.

There was a Paiute man living alone on top of a mountain near Reno, Nevada who grew more lonesome as days went by. There was also a woman, who lived far away to the east of that place. She was married to a man who abused her constantly. Finally, the abuser and his wife had a very long and bitter fight. To end the fight, the woman picked up a hatchet and hit the abuser on his head, killing him. She had heard that a man lived far to the west, who was kind and thoughtful, so she began walking to find him. Finally, after many days of walking, she saw foot tracks, larger than hers and surmised that they were the tracks of the man. She became afraid to go and meet him, but as her hunger and thirst mounted, decided to show herself to him. She stepped from behind a tree as he was walking toward her, and he called out to her. "Ho-ha, young woman! My name is Lone One, and I invite you to my home for food, drink and talk. I am very lonely and anxious to talk to someone. Would you accompany me to my lodge and eat with me?"

Being as hungry, thirsty and tired as she was, she agreed, and they walked toward his lodge. There, he prepared a soup, a few berries and nuts, along with a piece of dried venison for the two of them to enjoy. After the food, water, and the talking, the woman fell asleep, and the man moved to the other side of the lodge to enjoy his sleep. The next day they enjoyed more eating, drinking and talking, and in the evening the woman went to her side of the lodge, while the man moved closer to where she slept. After three nights, the man and woman slept together and married the following day. They had a number of children together, but the children never got along well together. They were always fighting between themselves, and the man became tired of the constant fighting. He told the woman that he was leaving, and went to the top of the highest hill and walked his way toward the seven stars of Pleiades in the Milky Way, disappearing behind the clouds above.

The woman began crying profusely, watching the children battle each other day after day, and the tears began flooding the valley below where she was sitting. The children left the area, some going east, others west, but after a time they came back to visit their mother. However, her tears had turned the valley into the Pyramid Lake, and she still sat in the middle. However, she had turned to stone. She still sits there, looking like a hooded woman with a basket beside her, northeast of Reno, Nevada, in the middle of Pyramid Lake. The legend says that her spirit followed her husband into the sky toward the west and into the Pleiades of the Milky Way.

The Paiute tribe is responsible for starting performances of the ghost dance, which is performed even to this time by many of the Native American and indigenous people. It was revealed to a Paiute man by the name of Wodziwod in a dreamcatcher he had in 1870, in which he dreamt that a great disaster would take place to eradicate the white man, and all of the dead Native American and indigenous people would return to life. This dance has been performed by many more tribes and bands, as they all have feelings of distrust for the white man who has stolen the lands of the red man. If and when this ever happens, supposedly all of the lands will be restored to the red men.

Chapter 3—Entry from the East

WHILE THIS WAS happening on the western part of North America, other groups of indigenous people were leaving a large island continent we now call Atlantis, which was supposedly positioned in the Atlantic Ocean between Europe and North America. Atlantis suffered from a number of volcanic eruptions with lava flowing over much of the land. About the same time as the Ice Age bridged part of the Arctic Ocean, the water in the Atlantic Ocean rose tremendously, completely covering the legendary island of Atlantis.

As the water rose, the people of Atlantis began retreating, some going east, and some escaping to the west. They each took whatever they could carry with them, including their beliefs, history, intelligence, language, and tools to forge new lives no matter where they would land. The people who fled eastward became people inhabiting Portugal, Egypt, Iran, Iraq, and Israel. Their history is better chronicled because of their early change to a written language before those of the people who fled westward. Of the people who sailed westward, it is said by the Mayan people of Mexico, they sailed to a new land in the Bimini Islands before sailing west to Florida. From there they crossed the Gulf of Mexico and settled in southern Mexico and northern Guatemala. Of all of the people who sailed west, their culture became the most advanced in the form of architecture, art, astronomy, engineering, mathematics, physics, and science.

The Mayan architecture mirrored the great pyramids of Egypt, the astronomical locations were similar to many found in the Mediterranean and European areas, and their scientific findings seemed to follow the same train of thought. Their cities were constructed with canals for transportation as well as water distribution, streets arranged around central squares containing what appeared to be religious gathering places, and the market places nearby. Their cities grew from the center outward, the first suburbs as it were, with the farmers living on the outskirts of the cities where the canals could water their crops. They grew much of their own foods, so agriculture was very important to them. Their calendars were the most accurate of any found in North and South America, and were found to have been originated before 500 BC and carried through to the supposed end of the world in December, 2012. Their written language was established around 700 BC, almost a thousand years before other cultures of North and South America. Mathematics were used by the Mayans in their art, architecture, engineering, medicine, and science. Then, around 750 AD, drought became the beginning of the end of their civilization as they left the large cities, formed smaller villages, and were defeated by the Aztec people who invaded from the north.

The Aztec civilization got their name from the places at which they lived before, possibly as far away as Aztalan, Wisconsin. As to their origination, there is a possibility that they crossed the Pacific Ocean from the Pacific island continent of Mu, and then crossing what is now the United States to the Mississippi River. They were nomadic people who followed the food chain, infiltrating down from their Mississippian homes. The many rivers and streams leading from the Mississippi River, and then on toward the southwest and Mexico would have been a natural route for them to follow. There were pyramidal mounds built at Aztalan, much as the pyramidal mounds built by the Mayan people. Also, the largest base of any of the pyramids built in North or South America are the Cahokia Mounds in southwest Illinois. The weather eventually broke down that pyramid into a high hill, but the outline of the huge base is still there. That is right next to the Mississippi River near Saint Louis, Missouri. It is extremely possible that the first people buried beneath that pyramid were the people who drowned when the rafts they used for crossing the river overturned in the wild, rushing water.

Following the Mississippi down to the area of New Orleans, then heading west alongside the coastline of the Gulf of Mexico through what is now the state of Texas, would have brought them to the very doorstep of what is now Mexico. Seeing another great culture ahead, they had the strength and will to become lord and master of that land and its people.

Aztec people overthrew the Mayan people and between slavery, inter-marriages, and human sacrifice almost annihilated the Mayan race. The Aztec culture grew in numbers and in stature until the 1500's AD, when the Spanish arrived and invaded the areas of Mexico, much of South America, and what became the southwestern United States. At that time, Montezuma was the leader of the Aztec empire, and Mexico City was their capital. The founding of that city is told in a legend that has been passed down through many centuries. According to the story, the Aztec people were looking for a place to build their capital city. They saw a bird, sitting on top of an arm of a Saguaro cactus, holding a snake lengthwise in its mouth in the middle of an island surrounded by water. The present national flag of Mexico depicts that very scene in the middle of its flag.

There are many legends and myths of the Mayan and Aztec people, but the mystery of the huge, magnificent buildings found in the areas occupied by them confound the imagination. The stone from which the buildings were constructed are so huge that it is impossible to lift them and place them within the structure as it was being built, even with the construction equipment used in present day construction. The preciseness of the interlocking is unbelievable, yet it is still there to witness these many hundreds of years later.

The Iroquois entered North America from the east arriving supposedly on the shores of North Carolina, originating from the lost island of Atlantis. According to one of their earliest legends, the spirit of the sky world flew over the earth. As he traveled over it, he found it beautiful. Before returning to his home in the sky, he called the five nations that made up the Iroquois nations together, and gave each of them a special gift.

He told them, "To the Mohawks, I give corn. To the patient Oneidas, I give the nuts and fruits of many trees. To the industrious Senecas, I give beans. To the friendly Cayugas, I give the roots of plants to be eaten. To the wise and eloquent Onondagas, I give grapes and squashes to eat and tobacco to smoke at camp fires." He gave them other advice, then quickly wrapped himself in a bright cloud and flew like a swift arrow to the sun. His return to his home in the sky world caused much rejoicing by his brother sky spirits.

The Iroquois, which was a portion of the people who were called the Wabanaki group, began walking north, following the birds and animals away from the heat and humidity of the Atlantic shoreline. Slowly but surely, the Iroquois made their way northward into what is now Canada, where they split up into a number of separate groups. The Iroquois groups were very warlike, and caused much harm to the many other groups living in Canada and the north Atlantic coast. The Iroquois became invaders and residents of the areas around Stadacona (Quebec), and Hochelaga (Montreal). A great prophet and leader of the Huron tribe, Deganawida, had a dreamcatcher one evening during the early 1380's, in which a combination of several of the fragmented groups would be combined in order to restore peace and strength to all of them. Unfortunately, Deganawida had a speech impediment that would

47

not allow him to reveal the details of his dream to all of the groups. The groups were the Mohawk, Cayuga, Oneida, Onondaga, and Seneca. A young follower of his by the name of Hiawatha was a very polished and persuasive speaker, who was able to get the five groups to join in a confederation sometime around 1390. Hiawatha had been born to the Onondaga group, but was adopted by the Mohawk people. To symbolize the formation of the league, Deganawidah planted the Tree of Peace in the Onondaga's (one of the five groups) territory in the middle of the various Iroquois tribes. Its roots of peace supposedly reached the four corners of the earth, its branches reaching into the sky. Placed on the top of the tree was the "Eagle who Sees Afar," and below the roots were buried all of the weapons of strife.

Then, in 1722 a sixth group, the Tuscarora was added to the Confederation to make it six Iroquois nations. Probably because of their superior numbers, and their hostility, they drove the Huron and Algonquin tribes from the area, almost wiping out the Algonquin tribe. In the years 1534, 1535, and 1541, a Frenchman explorer by the name of Jacques Cartier discovered and revisited both of the Iroquois villages mentioned above, and took the chief Donnacona and his sons captive, sailing back to France, where Donnacona's sons learned the French language and became interpreters upon their return to "the new world." The Iroquois confederation joined the British in the war against the French in 1756. The war became known as the seven year war, and that is when Canada became a British colony. Another very important date for Canada, Great Britain and the United States was June 15th, 1846 when Great Britain and the United States signed the Oregon treaty which determined the border between Canada and the United States west of the Rockies.

A great legend of the Wabanaki tribes is about the Seneca tribe which lived close to the Niagara Falls on the Canadian side. Niagara means "thundering waters" as the sounds made by the water cascading over the falls and falling on the cataract below is very loud. That tribe believed that the sound was made by a spirit, to whom a human sacrifice was made each year. A young woman was nominated by the people of the tribe to be the sacrifice each year. It was a great honor to be chosen and the year we are talking about was the year the chief's only daughter was chosen. The chief's wife had just died and he was very attached to his young, unmarried daughter. On the day that the sacrifice was to be sent over the falls in a white canoe, the chief was nowhere to be seen, but the canoe was prepared and the daughter got into it at the shore next to the village. As the canoe headed out from the shoreline, another white canoe left from behind a willow tree a short way upstream.

The chief who was the occupant of the other canoe paddled his way to the side of the canoe carrying his daughter to the falls, and both of them went over the falls at the same time. It is said by the Seneca people that the chief and his daughter were changed into pure spirits of strength and goodness. They live so far beneath the falls that the roaring is music to them. He is the ruler of the cataract, and she is the maiden of the mist.

Still other people came to North America from Atlantis, traveling by hollowed out logs, rafts, or boats they built. The people headed north, landing in the New England states, and becoming the Abenaki tribes, the Huron, Mi'kmaq, Malikeet, Passamaquoddy, and Penobscot families. They spoke an Algonquin-based language and were primarily fish and small animal eaters. It was these people, along with their cousin tribe of Paspahegh people that the first English arrivals met near Jamestown, Virginia in 1607. Long before that however, they had adversaries from the north who were the Iroquois people, actually also cousins of theirs. They fought over the hunting and fishing areas claimed by both, as well as the gathering places. Primarily speaking, the Abenaki people were agriculturists, as well as fish and meat eaters.

It is not strange that turkey became a staple for the first Thanksgiving as they were much easier to find and kill than the swift and elusive deer. For a number of years these people helped the new white arrivals with food and instructions on living in a hard, brutal land. However, within four years, fighting broke out between the two groups and the white men killed off their benefactors.

Some of the legends and myths originating from the people living in the eastern parts of North America follow. The Penobscot people tell of a young woman and her husband who had two children. A great famine came over the families of their village, and the woman began weeping heavily. Her husband asked her what he could do to help her to stop weeping, and she told him, "You must kill me, and then you will be able to provide food for our family and the rest of our clan. After killing me, have our two sons grab me by my hair and drag my body across that dry patch of earth until my skin is no longer a part of my body.

Four days after that is done, come back to see what has grown there." These words troubled the man greatly, and he went to everyone and everything with the same question, "What should I do?" The Great Spirit told him, "You must do as she asks." So, the next day, as the sun was straight above, he killed her, and told the boys to drag her body back and forth across the patch of ground she had designated. Four days later, when they returned to that area, rows of corn had grown, and became the main source of food from the ground. Other areas of ground were stripped of bushes, grass, and weeds, and kernels were planted there. Corn became a stable crop for the agriculturists.

One of the most beautiful and wondrous sights in all the world are the Northern Lights of the Arctic. The legend of how they were identified is a story told by all of the Abenaki (people of the First Light or people of Dawn-land). They are groups banded together to form the Wabanaki Confederation in the early 1600's. One of the Huron chiefs, long before that time, had a son whom he felt was different. The son would steal away from their home and not return for several days. The boy's absence caused the chief to tell his wife, "I am going to follow him to find out where he goes when he leaves our home." The following day the boy left the home and the chief followed him. The way was long and hard for the chief to keep up with the young boy. Eventually the chief became tired and sat down for a short time before trying to follow the boy again. All of a sudden, the chief seemed to lose his hearing, and a strange feeling came over him. Then he knew nothing. His eyes closed for a short while, and when he opened them, he found himself in a strange land. No sun, no moon, no stars, but the country was lit by a peculiar brightness. He saw many beings, but not people like his own people. They gathered around him and began talking, but he could not understand what they were saying. He was well treated by the beings, and noticed they were all watching a game being played that he had never seen before. The players all had lights on their heads and belts of various kinds that turned into rainbow colors as the game was played.

Just then, an old man came up to him and they began talking with each other, with the old man asking the chief if he knew where he was. The chief answered him by admitting he did not know where he was. The old man said, "You are in the land of Waa ban ban of the Northern Lights. I came here many years ago. I was the only one from the 'Lower Country', as we call it. But now there is a boy who comes to visit us every few days." The chief asked the old man, "How did you get here, and what tribe are you from"? The old man answered, "I follow the path called Spirits Path, through the Milky Way." The chief said, "That must have been the path I followed to come here. Did you have a queer feeling, as if you lost all knowledge along the way?" The old man said, "Yes, I did. I could not hear nor see." The chief said, "We did use the same path. Can you tell me how to return to my home in the Wabanaki camp? Also, I have been searching for my son who must be the boy who comes here to visit you. Can you tell me where I might find him?"

The old man told the chief, "Stay here and watch, you will see him playing ball." Then, the old man left to visit the many wigwams to invite everyone out to watch the ball game. The chief was happy to hear the news of his son, and soon the ball game began, with many beautiful colors covering the field.

The old man returned to the side of the chief, asking him, "Do you see your son playing?" "Yes, he is the player with the brightest light on his head. |" The two men went to see the chief of the

Northern Lights, and the old man spoke up saying, "The chief of Wabanaki of the Lower Country wants to return to his home and take his son with him." The chief of the Northern Lights called his people together, telling them of the wishes of the chief, and they all bid the chief and his son a good-bye. Two great birds were ordered to carry them back to their Wabanaki village. When they traveled the Milky Way, the chief felt the same strange feelings he had experienced when traveling that path earlier. When the chief's senses returned, he found himself and his son near their home. The chief's wife was happy to see him, as the son had arrived first, and told his mother that the chief would arrive shortly. Now her wigwam was filled with joy again.

An interesting legend of the Penobscot tribe is that of two young girls who would leave their homes in the early evenings. Looking up at the sky, they spoke of their wishes aloud to each other. The older of the two girls told the younger, "See that bright star up in the sky? I would choose to marry that one, for it is the brightest star in the sky." The younger girl saw the star the older girl had pointed to and said, "Oh! That would be a very nice view from where that star is, to look down and see all of the world as it is." A few nights later, the older girl left the village alone, walked downstream along that water.

She entered the forest a short way away from the village and became lost. Coming into a clearing in the forest, she met a handsome middle-aged man who asked her if he could help her. When she replied that she had become lost, the man said, "You had said the other evening that you would like to marry the brightest star in the sky. I am that star and would be happy to marry you, if you still want me." The girl nodded her head yes, and the man took her by the hand and the two of them were taken up by a cloud, far into the sky. Landing on the top of the sky, the man took her to his place in the sky, where she met other young girls who had married stars. She spent many happy days digging roots and preparing meals for her husband, the star, but was told never to dig the roots of the large green-topped bush next to the star's home.

The view from the sky was beautiful, and she was very happy living in the sky, but wondered many times about why she was warned not to dig the roots of that particular bush.

One day, her curiosity became the better of her, and she did dig for the roots of that forbidden bush. The hole she dug was the opening to a view above the village she had belonged to before she had married the star. Longing to see her family and friends below, she decided to assemble a rope that would extend all the way to the ground below by weaving the long, strong grasses growing in the nearby woods. After many moons, the girl thought that the braided strands would enable her to reach the ground. After beginning to lower herself toward the ground, she came to the end of the rope, and dangled for many hours, crying for help. An eagle heard her cries for help and flew beneath her, allowing the girl to ride its neck on the rest of the way to the ground. Arriving next to the stream, she walked back to the village where she met her young friend, and she told the young friend of her adventure, and the many things she had witnessed from the sky.

Many, many generations ago, a Penobscot chief and his family were invited to a big celebration at a Seneca village in Canada. He, his wife, and their young son prepared for the long trip to the Seneca village, which was undertaken by overland and river travel. Leaving their village on the first day, they began walking toward the Saint Lawrence River that would take them to the Seneca village. The father carried the canoe that would have to be placed in the river at the time they reached it, as it was to transport the family to the Seneca village. He was the leader of the three people. The mother carried the items they were going to need as they walked along the route. The son bounded ahead and the mother thought that he had caught up with his father, but no, when they stopped to camp overnight, the boy was not with either of them.

They began worrying and retraced their steps, trying to locate the boy. Unfortunately, they walked all the way back to their village without finding him. After arriving there, they sent out the men to search for him, but after several days of not finding him, the search was called off. All they could find were bear tracks near where the boy was last seen. The following spring, in the early morning hours, a female bear led the boy back into the village, and right up to the chief's teepee. The boy lifted the opening to the teepee and entered, waking his mother and father as the opening was lifted. The boy said he had slept the winter with the bear family. From that time onward, his family was known as members of the Bear clan, leaders of all the clans of that tribe.

The Passamaquoddy have a wonderful legend of the beautiful daughter of the chief of a village who was followed by every young man in their village. One, who was the strongest and bravest, asked her to marry him, but before they married, he wanted to go out to fight and win the fame and fortune to be able to care for the woman as long as they both would live. After asking her if she would marry him and no other, and her promise of fidelity for him alone, he left the village with other braves, searching for the foes that had entered the hunting areas that his clan had used for many summers. While their war party was gone, a rival group attacked the village in which he and the young girl lived and killed all of the old men who had stayed to protect the village, and enslaved the women and children. Because of her beauty, many of the attackers wanted to marry the beautiful girl, but she refused all of their advances.

When the young man and his braves returned to the area in which their village had been located, and seeing the destruction and the pathway the attackers had taken in leaving the area, the young man and his war party followed the trail and made plans to attack the village in which the attackers now lived. Although outnumbered, the surprise attack by the young man and his braves was successful, and he rescued the beautiful young girl and married her. Through his bravery, and the successful raid, he was voted to be the new chief of their village.

The Penobscot tribe tell the story of the Four Winds family, who lived in a cave near the top of a mountain in what is now Maine. They were responsible for making the air to circulate, water to flow, the tree branches to sway, the leaves to whisper, and the seasons to change. To cause the wind brothers to blow, they would stick their head outside the cave and blow. West Wind was the youngest, but the strongest. The north wind was the eldest, but softest, east wind the next softest, while the south wind had strong gusts, but not as strong as his brother, the west wind. Each would take turns blowing from the hole in the cave, but the north would always have to caution the west wind not to blow so hard that it would affect badly on their people, the Penobscot.

At that time, there was a giant beaver living in a lake near the Penobscot village. Sometimes, when the beaver was hungry, it would snatch a Penobscot man or woman fetching water from the lake, and take them to its home and eat them. There was a brave giant hunter living in that village who said that he would kill the giant beaver. He went down to the lake waiting for the giant beaver to appear. Suddenly, the beaver emerged from the lake and with one large snap of its mouth, engulfed the hunter into its mouth and swam back to its home. Once inside the stomach of the beaver, the hunter saw the remains of the people the beaver had captured and eaten. He took out his giant knife and started cutting the stomach of the beaver from the inside to the outside. As the water and air reached the remains of the people inside the stomach, they became alive and swam back to the shore of the lake to resume their lives among their families and clan.

The hunter became the hero for his village, and became a leader of his clan.

According to Passamaquoddy legends, the first shaman, or medicine man, was the son of a young woman who would walk through the woods, biting off a small piece from twigs she found along her walk. One of them was a special twig which impregnated her. At the proper time, she worried that her family would think badly of her as she was not married, but she did birth the baby boy. She made a small canoe, and, setting the boy in it, sent it floating down the river. Another young girl found the canoe floating near the shore of her village, and seeing the baby, took it to her home in her village. As the boy grew, it would walk down to the river each evening, and the next morning one of the young boys in the village was found to have died. A curious neighbor watched as the boy walked down to the river one night. The neighbor followed as the boy returned home, where he sat down and ate what looked like a small tongue. The following morning, the neighbor found another boy had died, and that his tongue was missing. The neighbor alerted her village of what she had seen, and it was decided that the boy had to be killed, and his body burned.

This was done, but the next day the boy returned to the village as a much larger boy. He promised he would not kill any other boys if the village would spare his life. Because of the supernatural events he had gone through, he became a great healer, and would heal people when asked. As he got older, he was approached by a young man. The young man wanted to become the one most favored by the women of his village. This was done, a potion was given to him, but the young man became very upset when all of the women began following him and constantly asked him for sexual favors. It became so harrowing, he could not get any sleep. He returned the love potion to the medicine man and left without it. Another young man went to the medicine man and asked to be granted a life that would never end. The medicine man said, "Go to a place in the forest where no trees or bushes are growing and just stand there." As he did that, he saw branches and twigs sprouting all over his body, and he became a tall cedar tree that stands there still.

According to the Mi'kmaq tribe of the New England area, before there were any humans on the earth, the animals and plant life were the only life. The four sacred elements, fire, rock, water and wind had been created first, and with them were the earth, moon, stars, and sun. Flowers, fruits, plants, trees, and vegetables were the second group of life to be created. The beautiful cat tails, roses, sunflowers, and tulips colored, and gave off a fragrance, covering the face of the earth. Grapes, raspberries, strawberries, and vegetable plants sprang to life and made the earth ready for occupancy.

Trees such as birch, butternut, elm, evergreen, hemlock, and maple began growing to the sky. This last grouping introduced medicines to be used by the people who followed later in creation. Then came the four-leggeds, winged and swimmers, including the bear, buffalo, deer, elk, mice, snakes, spiders and squirrels. The many types of birds of the air, bees, butterflies, eagles, hawks, hummingbirds, owls, parrots, robins, and vultures began stirring the air above the earth and pollinating the soil for new growth. The beavers, eels, many types of fish, sharks, and even whales began swimming in the waters of the creeks, lakes, rivers and oceans. These three orders lived together for a long while before humans became the fourth order of creation.

The Great Spirit wanted and expected all of his creations to live together responsibly, although he allowed the different life forms to change between animals, human and plant forms. Communication between the life forms was also permitted. Just as in the previous creation stories this did not work well, and there had to be several other worlds created with many generations of human beings living and dying while the Great Spirit attempted to correct things his creations did wrong.

Another group of people that left Atlantis were a group we now call the Cherokee. The Cherokee people of Oklahoma and North Carolina landed in North Carolina and remained there until the 1830's when many of their people were rounded up and were herded on their "Trail of Tears" by the white soldiers to the western side of the Mississippi River, which was considered to be "Indian Territory." There were some Cherokee who successfully hid out in the Smoky Mountains of North Carolina and were not found during the round-up and live there still. It is said by that group that at the beginning of the world a great buzzard was trying to dry the land below it, flapping its wings furiously, but occasionally it got too close to the land and caused deep valleys to form below high mountains, thus the Smoky Mountains.

Most of the people who were forced to march to the west were relocated in Oklahoma where they still reside in the northeastern part of that state. The Cherokee honored the four primary directions by colors with the north being blue because of the cold, the south as white because of warmth, east red due to the sun rising and the color of fire and blood, and west black as their beliefs were that is the direction of death. That proved true during the "Trail of Tears", for it is said that one-third of the total forced on the march died during that terrible time. Also, upon death, their spirits go to the west before going up to the stars in the Ursa Major, or Great Bear, constellation, if they lived on the red road (lived a life of goodness), or are sent back to the earth in another life form by the Great Judgment if they had lived on the black road, or the bad road.

One of the most widely told legends of the Cherokee is the story of the people killing too many of the animals for reasons beyond food, clothing, and shelter. The animals banded together and decided that they would get back at humans by infecting people with diseases. When the plants, who were friendly with the people, heard of this plan, they sought out the shaman and women, offering their bark, branches, flowers, leaves, and liquids as cures for those diseases. If the people were unsure of how to use them, the plants would direct them as to their use. Thus, flowers, grasses, mosses, plants, and trees became their first medicines. Many of those medicines are still used by not only indigenous people, but people all over the world.

There was a Cherokee village which held a special dance each first full moon. The Cherokee young men and young women looked forward to the occasion, and each of them hoped to find the person of the opposite sex to become their spouse. There were occasions that some young woman would appear at the dance, become what one might call the belle of the ball, and all of the young men would try to dance with her. They would all ask her to come to his teepee, but she would refuse each of them. There was one young man who decided to follow her home after the dance, but she didn't go toward their village, but rather toward the river next to the village. As she approached the river, she entered the river walking down deeper than her hips, past her shoulders, and finally above her head.

He had started in after her, but when she disappeared, he turned around and realized she was not a human being but a spirit playing tricks on the Cherokee men.

The Siouan-speaking people, becoming the Dakota, Lakota, and Nakota Sioux, who now live in North and South Dakota, Iowa, Minnesota, and Nebraska, also arrived on the shores of the Carolinas from Atlantis. Their nomadic ways led them to cross from the eastern seaboard to just beyond the Great Lakes area following the food chain. They were the hunters and gatherers, following the great herds of deer, bear, elk, wild pigs, and the other meaty animals they needed for their diets. Gatherers collected the flowers, grasses, leaves, mosses, mushrooms, plants and tree bark that was used as food, clothing and shelter.

The lives they led were not easy for any of them, young, old, pregnant, or sick. They followed rivers and streams, walking around or rafting across lakes, but staying close to water, a basic necessity of life. As they were constantly on the move, they formed shelters called teepees by cutting long, straight branches, forming a large circle on the ground, tying the top branches together with leather cords or thin branches, and covering the entire structure with animal hides to keep out the weather. The poles, cording, and coverings had to be transported to the next location for the next set-up.

As they approached mid-continent, they encountered a new, larger food source, buffalos. Since the buffalo always followed grassland, slowly grazing, their heads and eyes bowed down, it was easy for the Sioux hunters to surround a herd and pick out the ones they wanted to kill with their spears, and later, bow and arrows. The hunters would put wolf hides over their bodies and sneak up to the buffalo herds in order to find the largest buffalos to kill. The buffalo meat and hides were a great source for food, clothing, and protection for their shelters. The bones were used in making tools, kitchen utilities, and weapons. A short time later, they also came into contact with the Pawnee people who introduced the Sioux to bow and arrow hunting. They began using bows and arrows for hunting and fighting, and it became easier to hunt from longer range. The women accompanied the hunters so that they could butcher at the location of the kill. The buffalos led them to their present home areas.

Two young, handsome Sioux men were sent out as scouts to find where the buffalo were, so that the hunters could go out and shoot them with their bows and arrows. As they were searching, they saw a figure walking toward them at a far distance. They hid behind some bushes and waited for the figure to get closer that they might identify it. As it approached where they were hiding, they saw that it was a young, beautiful woman, carrying a bundle on her left arm. One of the young men said to the other, "She is so beautiful that I want her for my wife. I am going to go and get her and take her back to camp with me." As he grabbed for her, a whirlwind rose about them, and when it had subsided, the woman was standing alone with the man's bones piled at her feet.

She said to the other man, "I am on a journey to your people. Among them is a good man named Bull Walking Upright. I am coming to see him especially. Go on ahead of me and tell your people I am on my way. Ask them to move camp and pitch their tents in a circle, facing the north. There I will meet Bull Walking Upright and his people." The man went back to his camp and made sure everything was done according to her instructions. When she arrived, she met Bull Walking Upright, uncovering the gift she had for him. It was a red stone peace pipe, which had a small buffalo calf carved into the outside of the bowl.

She gave it to him and instructed him on the prayers that were to be said to the Great Spirit at the time the peace pipe was used, and that it was to be used at all of their ceremonies. She said, "When you are hungry, unwrap the pipe and lay it bare in the air. Then the buffalo will come where your hunters can easily kill them. Your families will have food and be happy." She also told them how to behave in order to live peacefully together. She taught them special prayers to be said to mother earth, and how to decorate themselves for ceremonies. She said, "The earth is your mother. So for special ceremonies, you will decorate yourselves as your mother does — in black and red, in brown and white. These are the colors of the buffalo also. Above all, remember this is a peace pipe I have given you. You will smoke it before all ceremonies. You will smoke it before making treaties. It will bring peaceful thoughts into your minds. If you will use it when you pray to the Great Spirit above and to mother earth, you will surely receive the blessings for which you ask."

After finishing her message, she turned and walked away. Outside the circle she laid down on the ground. She rose again as a black buffalo cow. Again she laid down, and rose as a red buffalo cow. A third time she laid down and rose as a brown buffalo cow. The fourth and last time she laid down, she rose as a spotless white buffalo cow, and, walking toward the north, disappeared over a far-off hill.

As the clan families followed the food chain, they found places that were reasonably comfortable, offered foods they cherished, and enabled them to lead lifestyles that became normal to them. From the pit houses dug by stone or bone digging tools, to tepees arranged in a big circle, to cave dwellings, to constructing log homes from the woods of trees, or by building their adobe homes with caliche mud, these people learned over time to form lives that were better than those of their forefathers.

They still found certain places that provided animals for hunting and they became familiar and knowledgeable in agriculture. Hunting was done year around and corn, melons, squash, and beans became their chief food crops, with tobacco necessary for many religious and social ceremonies. The people used the seasons for many purposes with the spring for planting their crops, summer for hunting and gathering, fall for harvesting the crops, after which they would get together with friendly groups near them, arrange marriages, exchange gifts, talk about things of mutual concern, trade goods that were needed or wanted between the groups, and conduct ceremonials of life and bury the dead. Preparing for the winter season of family togetherness time was also included at that time. Weaving baskets, blankets, and rugs, making and repairing of jewelry, weapons, cups, bowls, forks, spoons, and tool-making was done primarily during the winters. Preparing costumes for the ceremonies was done whenever time permitted. Storytelling by the oldest member of the family was set aside for winter evenings, and was a family method of teaching the children the history, legends, and myths of the clans.

The spring, summer and fall meant physical work, while the winter was a more relaxed time, if their family had adequately prepared with food, hides for blankets and shelter for protection. Winter would also usher in the ceremonies that were performed by the men in costumes that represented the deities they worshipped. Each man would participate in ceremonies of his mother's family clan, not with his wife's clan.

As many groups were matriarchal in family life, the woman owned the home in which the family lived. Marriages were allowed only when the two partners were from two separate clans, with the man paying a dowry to the woman's family before the marriage was approved and then he would live with the woman's family. Children of the marriage would become part of the mother's clan, be educated by her brothers, sisters and grandmothers of that side of the family, and the man would continue to function in ceremonies of his own clan, not those of his wife's clan. He would have no responsibility of teaching his own children but would help teach the children of his sisters.

Divorce was allowed and easily performed if the woman took all of the husband's possessions and put them outside the home. The husband would have to pick up his possessions and take them back to his mother's home and begin living there again. If the mother was deceased, he had to go to a sister of his to live, or he had to leave the community to seek another home. This is common to many matriarchal-based bands and tribes. It seems foreign to us as it is usually the woman who changes her last name to her husband's last name and is called Mrs. _____ in our society.

Chapter 4—Finding the Right Place to Live

THERE WERE OTHER groups of people leaving Siberia who used large handmade, carved-out wooden canoes to hunt whales and other sea life, who settled on islands between Siberia and North America along the Alaskan and Canadian coasts. Some settled on the Haida Gwaii Islands off of the British Columbia coastline of the Pacific Ocean.

These people sailed across just after the time the water melted the ice and covered the land bridge, about 14,000 years ago. This group formed the Heitsuk Nation, became great hunters and fishermen, and formed villages that have just recently been discovered on other islands off of the coast of British Columbia, Canada. In order to display friendship when meeting other people in their canoes, they raise their paddles upright as they approach each other.

The First Nation tribes of Canada are so very important in history, for they fought with and against the British, French and our own American people in wars going back to the 17th century. But long before those battles, languages originating from the Aleut and Athapaskan people, and many other groups of those who crossed the Bering land bridge, became those used by people who spread across what is now known as North America. The Aleut language is spoken by the Aleut and Eskimo people of Alaska, the Aleutian Islands, and eastern Siberia.

The Athapaskan language was brought from Siberia down to the Southwestern United States by the Apache and Navajo people, in the states of Arizona, Colorado, New Mexico, Texas, and Utah. In fact—as mentioned earlier—during the Second World War, the Navajo code talkers confused the Japanese by using that language, wherein the meanings of words that are essentially the same are specified by the tones of voice used in speaking the language. The Athabaskan language is still spoken in the Apache and Navajo reservations of Arizona, as well as along the Siberian, Alaskan and British Columbia coastlines, and the Paiute reservation along the Oregon coastline. However, prior to the white man arriving on the shores of North America, the language most spoken by the indigenous peoples of North America was the Cree language.

The migration across what is now Canada, and down into what is now the United States of America took many centuries and more generations than we can begin to count. Each movement was predicated on finding or following the food, shelter, safety, and hoped-for comfort chains. Beautiful, leafy, tall forests, colorful valleys, high rugged mountains, and the unending brooks, lakes, rivers and streams led to food sources and shelter these wandering people sought. Finding places that offered what they needed, they would stop and plan a life for themselves and their families. Everyone has dreams, and these people had them too.

When setting up villages, an organization of government took place. There were always leaders, hunters, gatherers, medicine men and religious leaders called shamans to guide the members of the groups. Hunting and fishing were done by the men, while cooking, cleaning, cutting and curing hides of animals, and gathering edible

64

berries, flowers, leaves, mushrooms, and roots was mostly done by the females. Working with sand, stone and wood, and weaving fibers of animal furs, grasses, and vegetation were done by the men. The elders were most often honored as leaders because of their experience, knowledge, and patience. However, as possessions in land, shelter or other valuables became part of their family wealth, most of the people became matriarchal.

The Rocky Mountains became the area of which the people were afraid. The peaks reached almost to the sky, and sometimes, when the clouds encircled the peaks, the people were afraid to go beyond there, not knowing what to expect. The snow and ice were not conducive for climbing or walking during the winters, and summers lasted only a short part of the year.

A great story about the Rocky Mountains is the legend of the young Two-Horned Mountain goat ram who claimed he could climb any mountain. He constantly looked for the tallest mountain, climbed it, and returned to his proud father and the family. He saw the tallest peak of the Rocky Mountains and began climbing it. When he got to the top he found that there was no room for him to turn around and begin to descend from that peak. The Great Spirit saw his situation and told him, "I see that you cannot go down from this peak to your father, family, and village. So I will make you a star that your family and all creation will see, and they will call you the North Star. You will never have to move, and people for all time to come will use you in navigating from one point on mother earth to another." Thus, we have the North Star which we use to travel from one point to another.

It was far easier for the Apache and Navajo groups to follow the western edge of those mountains southward, and besides, they could find food and water where they collected at the bottom of the slopes. So much land and so few people! This became the paradise they had been looking for with the many animals, birds, plant life and trees growing straight and tall, available for food, clothing and shelter. Each group sought out and found the area they wanted to call their own. This worked out fine until a group decided to encroach on another's elected territory. Battles began between people of different groups, with the invaders' surprise attacks often defeating the people who had lived in the region for a long period of time and considered it their own. The two groups would then become natural enemies, such as the Cree and Iroquois, the Apache and Pima, the Navajo and Hopi. Some of their war stories have made it through history and legends.

As the clans separated, new language patterns were established with the Cree, Inuktitut, and Ojibway people crossing over the Rocky Mountains toward the east, their languages and their many dialects spoken among the First Nation groups in Canada. In what was to become the United States, Algonquin, Caddo an, Keresan, Siouan, Uto-Aztecan and Zuni were among the many languages and dialects used throughout the bands and tribes, some of which originated in other places of this world. Many of the languages used have become nearly extinct as the English, French and Spanish languages became more universal.

Now, as we look at the various parts of North America, we find the largest contingent of Cree living in Canada, and the Navajo tribe being the largest, and possibly the richest, tribe in the United States. The Navajo Nation's reservation is as large as the entire state of West Virginia, and larger than four other individual states. It covers over 17 million acres, a good share of northeastern Arizona, northwestern New Mexico and southeastern Utah, and a very small section of southern Colorado. In fact, although the Hopi people and their ancestors are considered to be Native Americans, roamed the entire continents of North and South America during their migration long before the arrival of those who came across from Asia or other parts of the world, their assigned reservation is very small and smack in the middle of the Navajo reservation of northeastern Arizona.

This causes many problems between the two tribal councils and residents. By the way, the Hopi Nation is the only tribe in Arizona that does not, at this time, own a casino. They work very hard caring for sheep, goats, cattle, horses, and dogs, as well as their agricultural products. Their artisans do make beautiful ceramic figures, baskets, Kachina dolls, jewelry, and other crafts as well. Their lives are not easy, but their faith in the goodness of the Great Spirit allows them to carry on their primary mission of caring for mother earth and living in peace and harmony. Until just recently, parts of the Navajo and Hopi reservations were not even provided with electricity. That connection took place during the late spring of 2019.

Having walked southward into what is now northeast Idaho, where they decided to set up a camp for the winter, two of the men of the Mescalero Apache band became ill. Not realizing that they had the power to heal these two men, the Mescalero band of men were standing around the two men who were lying inside the kiva one evening when the voice of the Great Spirit asked the assembled men why they stood doing nothing for the two sick men.

Four of the men each of whom stood to the north, south, east and west of the sick men heard the next words of the Great Spirit, who said "Two of you men chant songs of prayer to me, while two strike the drums in my honor. Then, tomorrow lay your hands on the sick men and they will recover." After the four men had performed the requested actions, the men returned to health the following day. And that was the origin of the curing ceremony performed on the sick members of that band for many years thereafter. Even now, the traditional curing ceremonies are used by some of the people who are considered to be shamans, or medicine men.

Upon moving from one area to another, the Apache groups would send out scouts to find the best places to find food or for settling down for short periods of time. These scouts were sometimes alone, or a pair would go out together. As a lone scout approached an area of northern Arizona, he came across an area that showed footprints in the sands of a small lake. The footprints were of two people walking together, and a trail of blood followed between their footsteps. This meant either of two things, one of them was injured or they were transporting a dead animal, probably food for their clan. He followed the tracks, staying far enough behind that he would not be spotted, but caught up to the pair within a few hours. It was getting dark and the two hunters did indeed have a large buck deer they were carrying back toward their clan's location. Eventually they stopped, behind a line of trees, and started a small campfire. He watched as they began eating what appeared to be a rabbit stew with a few acorns that had dropped from one of the trees above. They had been talking in a language the scout did not understand, but from the gestures of the men, he thought that they were still a day away from their camp.

Waiting for darkness to hide his movement from the pair, he carefully and quietly approached the line of trees behind which the pair had settled down to sleep. After hearing the snores of the two men, he slipped between the trees, going to his knees next to the man closest to the tree line. He covered the man's mouth with one hand and plunged his knife into that man's stomach, tearing it upward toward his heart killing that man quietly. No sound escaped the victim. Rising from his knees, he moved over next to the other man, and killed that man, too. After scalping both of the dead men, he hefted the large buck onto his back and started walking back toward the place where his clan had camped. He knew there would be rejoicing at his camp when he brought the buck and the scalps he took while procuring the meat. Yes, for the time he would be a hero, and perhaps win an eagle feather for himself. The eagle feathers were awarded to those men for their bravery and doing good things for the clan. This event was a first between an Apache scout and two Hopi hunters.

As the Apache people began moving southward, they came into contact with other people called pueblo people, whom we met in my previous book called "When the Spirits Move." As you will recall, these pueblo people were hunters, gatherers, and agriculturists, not fighters

The Apache people settled to the east and south of their cousins, the Navajo, in northeastern New Mexico, eastern and southern Arizona, and northern Mexico, becoming known as

Coyotera, Jicarilla, Lipan, White Mountain, Mescalaro Chiricahua, and Yaqui Apache nations.

The Jicarilla Apache people have a story that tells how and why they live where they do, which is in northeastern New Mexico. As the Jicarilla clans followed the food chain, they moved in a circular motion around the area now called the Four Corners, where Arizona, Colorado, New Mexico and Utah meet. As they continued circling in that area, the Great Spirit asked them what they were doing, and what they were looking for. They said, "We are looking for the middle of the earth." So the Great Spirit led them to an area near what is now Taos, New Mexico, where they have lived since that time.

Another legend of the Jicarilla band of Apaches tells the story of how the animals first obtained fire. All of the animals wanted fire to warm themselves during the cold evenings in the desert, but the only place that had fire was the village of the fireflies. The only animal smart enough to think of a plan to get the fire from the firefly village was the fox. He approached the village of the geese, and asked them if they could teach him how to fly.

After much persuasion by the fox, the geese consented to try to teach the fox how to fly. They gave him an extra set of wings, with which he covered his back and inserted his forelegs in the bands beneath the wings, and said he was ready for his first flight. The geese cautioned him not to open his eyes, but to follow the sounds of their calls as they flew ahead of him. As they gained altitude, the fox thought of which direction they headed, which was over the firefly village, and started counting the amount of time it would take to position himself over the village before opening his eyes. Sure enough, as he opened his eyes he saw the village directly below him. Down, down, down he fell, right into the middle of the firefly village.

All of the fireflies saw his fall and came running over to see if he was alright. Since he was not hurt in the fall, he asked them how he could leave the village, and they showed him a cedar tree whose branches would bend over when requested, and allow him to be catapulted over the wall when he was ready to leave. They were having a celebration dance that evening and invited the fox to participate. As the fireflies danced, they flew close to the fire, and the fox followed the dancers until he could reach the flames. Then, in a twinkling of an eye, the fox had grasped some of the flames, run to the tree, and requested the tree to bend down, and was catapulted over the wall and toward the waiting animals outside the firefly village. And that is how the animals got fire.

Favorite hunting grounds and gathering places were traditional to both the Hopi and Navajo, and essential to life itself. Agriculture helped many groups feed their growing clans, and marriages between various members of different clans helped to grow their communities. Even now, a member of a clan, such as the Turtle clan, is not permitted to marry anyone from the same clan. But when one group infringed on another's chosen area, wars between the two parties erupted. The stronger party took over the territory, until defeated by a stronger foe, or until the winner moved on to another area.

These types of encroachments took place between the pueblo people and the Apache and Navajo people entering the Southwest from the north and northeast. All were searching for food and a place in which they could feel secure. The Navajo found such a place in the four corners area of the now states of Arizona, Colorado, New Mexico and Utah. Four mountains surrounded them—Mount Blanca in the La Plata Mountains of Colorado to the northeast, Mount Taylor known to them as Turquoise Mountain in New Mexico representing the southeast, the San Francisco Peaks representing the west, and Mount Hesperus to the east. These were sacred to the Navajo, who felt protected by them.

There were two young boys born to the first Navajo mother. The oldest boy was the son of the sun god, while the second boy was the son of the water spirit. There was a monster that fell in love with the mother, but she wanted nothing to do with the monster. The monster saw children's footsteps in the sand around the mother's hogan, and wanted to kill them so he could be the closest being to the mother. The mother was aware of the monster's ideas and hid the boys before the monster came around. As the boys grew, the mother taught them how to shoot arrows from bows, and after making one bow and several arrows, she took them out for practice. They kept asking their mother how and when they could see their fathers, and finally she told them that their fathers lived far to the west, beyond the area where the canyon walls would squeeze the life out of anyone who tried to pass through, beyond the great canyon that was very deep, and beyond the big waters to the west. Finally, they were old enough and brave enough to leave the mother's Hogan and begin their quest to find their fathers.

They walked for many days before they came to a small house. They knocked on the doorway, and the door was opened by a very old and small woman, who said that she was Spider Woman. They asked whether she knew where to find their fathers and she told them it was far west of where they found her. She gave them some food and prayer sticks, then sent them on their way. They came to the narrow canyon walls and raised the prayer sticks in front of them as they passed through. Next they approached the deep wide canyon, and after walking around it looking for a way to reach the other side, they raised their prayer sticks to the sky, and said a prayer they had been taught by Spider Woman, and a rainbow that spanned the canyon appeared.

They climbed onto the rainbow and walked across the top of the canyon before walking again on the other side. They finally came to the big waters (we now call the Pacific Ocean). Once more they took out the prayer sticks and repeated the prayer that the Spider Woman had taught them, and the rainbow appeared and led them straight to the sun god and the water spirit's home.

Legends and myths about animals were always very popular, being told by the elders and storytellers in early evenings during the wintertime in many villages and many tribes. The coyote was oftentimes the hero, or the butt of the stories. A coyote went to live with the bear clan at one time, but often went off during the night to steal food from neighboring clans. This time he stole corn from the fields of the eagle clan, and after several nights of stealing, the members of the eagle clan set a trap for the coyote. They formed a figure of a man made of pitch, and set it on the road leading from the bear clan's village to their corn fields.

As the coyote approached the figure, he demanded that it get out of the way so that it could pass by. The pitch figure did not move, so the coyote warned it that it would hit the figure with its right front paw, which would kill the figure. When the figure did not move, the coyote slammed its paw into the pitch figure. The paw stuck in the pitch. The coyote warned the figure that its left front paw was more powerful, and it would strike the figure with it in order to kill the pitch figure. Again the paw stuck in the pitch, and the coyote used its two rear legs to kick the figure with the same results to its legs. The coyote's tail was next, and finally the coyote bit into the pitch, which meant it was completely attached to the figure.

The next morning a member of the eagle clan found the coyote stuck to the pitch figure, tied up the coyote and pulled it from the figure's clutches. Taking the coyote to his shelter, he tied it to the side of the shelter and began boiling water in which to scald the coyote's hide. A short while later, a fox came around the shelter, and asked the coyote what it was doing tied to the shelter. The coyote lied and said that the clan member was cooking him a nice dinner with lots of corn, and potatoes. If the fox would release him, the coyote would tie the fox to the shelter, so that the both of them could enjoy the meal.

Of course, after the fox was tied to the home, the coyote ran off, and the fox was scalded so badly that its skin turned red. Trying to get even, the fox went to the bear clan's home asking for the coyote. Told that the coyote always went for a cool drink every evening at the nearby stream, the fox surprised the coyote while it was taking a drink. Jumping on its back, the coyote looked down into the water seeing the watercress in the ripples of the water. The coyote suggested that the two drink all of the water so that they could eat the watercress. The two of them began drinking the water, but after a short time the coyote faked drinking while the fox continued. When the fox could drink no more, the coyote ran off, with the fox too full of water to follow.

Another Navajo legend has to do with parenting their children. Those Navajo people, living in what is now called Canyon de Chelly (pronounced canyon de Shay), use the tall needle rock known as Spider Rock, located within the canyon, to discipline their children by telling them that spider woman lives up there. And when she sees naughty children living below, she climbs down the huge spider web, grabs the child, and climbs up the web, after which she pulls the web up to the top where it remains until the next naughty child is seen. The children taken up by spider woman are never seen again, and when people look upon the needle from the upper rim of the canyon, there is white dust or dirt on the top of the needle, which the parents tell their children are the bone remnants of the naughty children.

Many legends and myths became part of many tribes throughout the continent. For an example, the next legend is much the same as the Tlingit legend told earlier in this book. This one has a specific location for the bird's home, unlike the Tlingit legend. A Navajo legend tells of a giant bird, which lived in what is now called the Four Corners of Arizona, New Mexico, Colorado, and Utah. The giant bird was a danger to the Navajo people. Their legend tells of the bird scooping up people, carrying them up to the top of a tall needle on what is now called Shiprock in New Mexico.

The bird would eat the people and leave their bones on the top of the needle rock for her baby chicks. Finally, one of the hero-men of a nearby village told the people of the village that he would kill the bird. He laid down on the trail between the village and the tall needle rock pretending to be dead. The bird swooped down and thinking the man was dead, picked him up in his talons and carried him up to the nest above. The bird thought it would cook the man before eating him, so left to get the kindling and wood for the fire, but while it was gathering the fuel for the fire, the man rose and captured a baby chick and asked where the giant bird's heart was to be found. The chick told him it was in the back of the bird's left ankle, and so the man grabbed a knife and waited for the bird to return, hiding behind the doorway on the right side. As the bird entered the doorway, the man jabbed the knife into the left ankle, killing the bird. He released all of the people who had been captured and brought them back to their villages.

Most of the legends and myths told by the elders and storytellers of the Hopi, Acoma, Pima, Tohono O'odham, and Zuni tribes were about the days before the Apache and Navajo people entered the southwest. The stories of mystical animals, ghosts, giants, mysteries, and spirits were orally passed down through many generations, and were used in educating, entertaining, and explaining the ways of life of ancestors they never knew. All of them began with the phrase, "Many, many, moons ago, long before you and I were born, ---------."

"Many, many, moons ago, our village was visited by traveling traders, who brought items from other areas of the world that we did not grow, hunt or gather in our areas. There were birds called parrots, dressed in many beautiful colors—red, green, blue, brown, yellow, and black—that could sing and talk in beautiful tones that imitated our songs and speech. These would be traded to our ancestors who wanted them for their beautiful feathers and our ceremonies. Foods from faraway places, stone and wood pieces not found in our area formed into bowls, baskets, blankets, forks, hatchets, jewelry, knives, and weapons were brought in and traded for items we had that those people faraway could not find or make in their areas.

It was important that these traveling traders came to tell us of the ways other people lived, and some of the things they did that would help us in how we lived. These traveling traders also helped us grow our clans and villages by fathering children at the request of our clan elders, as they provided new blood, rather than allowing brothers and sisters to have babies together. One such traveling trader was a man named Kokopelli, a man who came from a village many moons to the south of us here. He is considered by our clan as a traveling trader and god of fertility, as he was responsible for many children to be born to our clans. His blood may run through your body even though his life was over many, many moons before even your grandfathers and grandmothers were born. He visited many villages from the great waters where the sun goes to sleep to the Petrified Forest where the wooden logs turned to stone. He walked from beyond where the bean people (Papago) live to the south of us to the area beyond the sipapuni in the depths of the huge canyon.

His service to all of the Great One's creations and creatures was left on rocks in the form of petroglyphs and pictographs throughout the areas in which he served. His is the figure of the bent-backed man carrying a flute, and a pack on his back, and his name is Kokopelli." This is an often-told legend in the families of the pueblo people.

The story of how butterflies came into this world is from the Pima people, a pueblo people about whom I wrote in my previous book "When the Spirits Move." Once upon a time, many years ago, people of the Pima Nation lived just south of where the city of Phoenix is situated now. A group of children were playing outside their homes, throwing sticks and stones into the air and chasing them as they came down onto the earth. The "Great Spirit" was watching them and thought to himself, "I can do better than that." He picked a rawhide bag out of nowhere, began filling it up with different colored natural things, such as flowers, feathers, and even a caterpillar.

He shook the bag and opened the top to let out what was inside. Butterflies began to fly, darting left and right, up and down, and the children began to chase them, screaming loudly in their joy. The parents came running out of their homes to see what the excitement was all about, and seeing the colorful butterflies, began chasing them themselves.

As attacks became more frequent, and more of the Apache and Navajo groups became involved, the pueblo people moved to areas that would provide water and be more defendable. The pueblo people found caves in cliffs and other places to build their homes.

Many found high hills from which they could see advancing groups and prepare for battle. Food and shelter were still the prime requirements for both groups, and both were willing to fight for their families' lives. Most of these incursions occurred in the mid-13th century, which was also the time of a very severe drought. The pueblo people from various areas of the southwest became known as Anasazi (the name given them by the Navajo's which meant old enemies who are no more), Salado (people who lived along the Salt River), and according to the Pima and Tohono O'odham people, the Hohokam (old people who have vanished).

The Anasazi were the forefathers of the Hopi, Acoma, and the people who lived in what is now northern Arizona and central New Mexico. The Salado and Hohokam people were the later Pima and Tohono O'odham (Papago, or bean eaters), people of today. The Zuni were the people who settled on the area alongside the Zuni and the Rio Pescado Rivers, near the eastern edge of what is now Arizona and the western edge of what is now New Mexico.

Gradually, the Apache and Navajo took over the huge areas that once were the pueblo people's territory. The pueblo people never owned it, they had just used it. Ownership was granted to the indigenous and Native American people in the 1870's when they were granted by the U.S. government territories called reservations. The territories are huge, but the land doesn't offer much in the way of good farming land, at least not in Arizona.

The Navajo people found coal beneath some of their land, but the coal mines are being shut down by governments because of the harm they do to our environment. That is why many tribes and bands petitioned the states to be able to own and operate gaming casinos. Some of the indigenous people living in Oklahoma on reservations have found oil beneath their reservation lands. These are just two of the ways they are receiving justice from the American and Canadian governments.

Now for a few legends of the indigenous people of mid-continental United States. This next area is the Great Lakes area, and the many tribes that made that their home after being forced south by the warring Iroquois tribes of southeastern Canada.

Some of the people who had originally stopped for a while in central and southeastern Canada, then continued on southward were the Ojibwa, Ho-Chunk of the Siouan language, and Mohicans, and other clans of their bands. As they entered North America from Atlantis by way of the Atlantic Ocean, they called themselves the Anishinaabe people, meaning original man, or first people. The Ojibwas split into many separate bands, including the Bad River Chippewa, Lac Courte Oreilles (originally called Winnebagos), Lac de Flambeau, Menominee, Oneida, Potawatomi, Red Cliff, and Saint Croix. Actually, Chippewa means "puckered toe moccasins."

The legend for the Ojibwas tells of their movement following the Saint Lawrence to the area of the Great Lakes. They had been told by the Great Spirit to search "for the place where food grows on water." That place was found on Madeline Island near the south shore of Lake Superior, and the mainland south of the island. The Bad River Chippewa band lived on the island first, then moved to the mainland near the confluence of the Bad and White Rivers in Wisconsin. One of their main buildings in each of the villages was a large, round ceremonial house in which marriages, naming of children, pipe ceremonies, and sweat lodge ceremonies were held by the Grand Medicine Society.

The Lac Courte Oreilles, or Winnebagos, were part of the band that found the wild rice on Madeline Island, and stayed there for a period of time before moving to the mainland with the Bad River Chippewas, and settled south of where the Bad River people settled. During one of their earliest days living there, a child died, and the band moved away. But the child's parents refused to leave, and when the band returned to that place, they found the family living well with the wild rice and white-tailed deer in good supply. It was the Bear clan that moved back there.

Their most sacred emblem is the drum. The circle of its sides represents a life cycle, with its wood and hide frame representing honesty and sharing in the natural world. Because it is made from animals and plants, it is a reminder that all of the elements making up the drum are dependent on each other. Another band that split off from the Ojibwa group is the Sokaogon band of Ojibwa. After leaving Madeline Island, they began living near the entrance to the Wolf River and harvested wild rice, hunted and fished those waters. They are also known for their art of making moccasins.

The Red Cliff band of the Lake Superior Chippewa Indians and the Saint Croix Chippewa were parts of the Anishinaabe of the Ojibwa group that initially were located in south central Canada, then moving on to northeastern New York State. It was there that the Ojibwa bands heard the aforementioned warning from the Great Spirit that if they didn't move to search for a place where "food grows on water", they would be faced with destruction. As they moved, they found wild rice growing in the waters of Madeline Island, but both the Red Cliff and the Saint Croix bands moved to the mainland, just as the Bad River, Lac Courte, and Sokaogon had done. They all found separate areas in which to live, but became part of the "council of the three fires."

The Menominee tribe are the oldest continuous inhabitants of Wisconsin. Their clan system designated each member as a person dedicated to hold certain responsibilities to the tribe. The clans were the Bear, Eagle (Thunderer), Crane, Wolf and Moose. The Bear clan's responsibility was to be speakers and law keepers, the Eagle (Thunderer) clan kept peace and justice, The Crane clan were the architects responsible for building and maintaining village structures, the Moose clan provided security for the village, and the Wolf clan were the hunters and gatherers. Before the Ojibwa people arrived in the area, the Menominee people hunted, fished, and gathered from Green Bay down the Wolf River, into Lake Winnebago, all the way to northern Illinois—around ten million acres west of Lake Michigan.

The Menominee became famous for respectfully harvesting salmon that migrate from Lake Winnebago to spawn in the Wolf River. Three of the most important religious parts of the Menominee nation's beliefs are the big Drum ceremony to heal both mental and physical illnesses, the responsible harvesting of sturgeon fishing, and the use of maple syrup from the many maple trees within their reservation. The big drum ceremony calls the sturgeon back to their traditional spawning grounds in the Wolf River and helps in the curing of various illnesses. The drum beat represents the heartbeat of mother earth and nature.

The Oneida tribe was a latecomer to Wisconsin, arriving near Green Bay in 1824 from northeastern New York. They were part of the Iroquois Confederation of Five, the Seneca, Oneida, Cayuga, Mohawk, and Onondaga, which later added the Tuscacora tribe to make it the Six Nation Confederacy. The Oneida people were known for their "long houses", some of which were as long as one hundred yards, made from arched maple sapling frames with elm bark shingles covering the outside, and moss as insulation.

The people who lived within the "long houses" were of the Bear, Turtle and Wolf clans. Also, this tribe is matriarchal, meaning the woman is the head of the family, and owns the property on which they live. The Oneida people were hunters and trappers, being very astute fur traders, and siding with the British against the French during the wars between the two European nations. However, during the Revolutionary war, the Oneidas became allies of the American forces. "Long houses" of today are used exclusively for ceremonies. Over time, the Oneidas became great agriculturists, using corn, squash, and beans as their principal crops, knowing that growing together they sustain the earth, alone they withdraw nutrients from the earth. Their famous white corn is their most noted crop.

The Potawatomi tribe originated in an area north of Lake Huron and Lake Superior. They were great hunters, gatherers and trappers. Their trading with the French was prosperous until other European people began moving into the areas below those lakes. There was a meeting at which the Ojibwa, Ottawa, and Potawatomi groups made a pact that allowed the Ojibwa the responsibility of keeping the faith, the Ottawa keeping the trade between the three open, and the Potawatomi became known as "the keepers of the sacred fire." Together they were known as "the Council of the three fires." The symbol of the Potawatomi is a circle within which is an Indian kneeling before a roaring fire, with three eagle feathers suspended from the bottom third of the circle confirming the pact between the three tribes.

Many of the leaders of the above groups have been honored by names of cities named after them. There were chief Oshkosh, chief Kewaskum, chief Decorah, chief Menominee of the Potawatomi (who actually lived in Indiana), and many cities containing clan and group or tribe names such as Oneida, Sauk City, Fox Lake, and Suamico and Little Suamico (one of the interpretations is yellow beaver tail), and many, many more. There is also a Kickapoo Valley in the southwestern part of Wisconsin, but there is no reservation for them anywhere near there. The Kickapoo reservations are in Kansas, Oklahoma, and Texas. Kickapoo ("those who are standing here and there", or "wanderers") were originally hunters and gatherers in the southern Great Lakes region, but were warred upon by Iroquois tribes and pushed to wander through Kansas, Oklahoma, Texas, and even into Mexico.

The Lac Courte Oreilles (Winnebago) tell as one of their legends the story of the boy stolen by the Thunderbirds. A young boy found a young pigeon hawk which had hurt its wing, could not fly nor find food for itself. The boy faithfully took care of the bird and fed it until it could begin flying on its own again. The boy and his friend went hunting for birds in the woods near their home one day. They became separated when fog rolled into the area in which they were walking. A thunderbird flying above saw the young boy walking all alone and decided to take the boy prisoner and fly him up to its home on top of a high hill. Upon arriving there, the thunderbird tied the boy to the floor with the plan of starving him until the boy had nothing left in his stomach and then it, and its family would eat the boy. The young pigeon hawk was a constant visitor to the thunderbird's home and found the boy tied to the floor of the thunderbird's home, and very hungry.

The pigeon hawk brought food to the boy when the thunderbird was not home, and the thunderbird became suspicious after a few days. The pigeon hawk was refused admittance, but temporarily pushed its way into the home. The thunderbird pushed the pigeon hawk toward the fire pit and singed some of the feathers of the pigeon hawk. In order to help its friend, the boy, the pigeon hawk went to the chief of the thunderbirds, chief Big Black Hawk, telling him the situation. Big Black Hawk flew with the pigeon hawk to the home of the offending thunderbird and seeing the boy tied to the floor became angry and untied the boy.

The chief and pigeon hawk saw that the boy was weak from not eating well for a period of time, and the chief took the boy to its home where the boy was fed and treated well. After regaining his strength, the chief and pigeon hawk suggested that the boy return to his village and his friends. He was flown back to the area of the woods where he had been abducted, and found his friend, who had been returning there each day in hopes of finding the boy, and they both returned to their village.

The Illini tribe were early inhabitants of Illinois, Indiana, Iowa, Michigan, and Missouri. One of their chiefs, Chief Ortega, was a fearless leader, but there was a huge storm-bird that lived in a cave across a small lake from where the tribe lived. The storm–bird would attack individuals who walked alone near the shore whenever it would see one. The people were scared to leave their village unless someone was with them.

It became so bad that the council had a meeting about what to do about the problem. Chief Ortega said that he would go alone out to the shoreline if there were archers that would hide in the bushes until the bird arrived, then they could kill the bird with the many arrows they would shoot at it. After the archers had been positioned to each side of where he would stand, the chief stepped out and waited for the storm-bird to exit its cave and fly toward him.

The archers used much patience before letting loose a large number of arrows that hit the bird, killing it. A large petroglyph on the side of a boulder near the area of the event was carved, but through time, and carelessness, the petroglyph was destroyed. The Illini were pushed westward by invaders, eventually moving to

Kansas and Oklahoma. One of the most famous chiefs was Chief Pontiac, whose name was used for the city of Pontiac, Michigan.

These legends and myths have been written of the people who came into North and South America, and tell of how these people overcame some of the hardships they lived through which stuns the imagination. Now we have the opportunity to look back on their struggles, sometimes not even recognizing some of the problems they confronted. I hope this book explains some of the problems they faced in carving out a life for themselves and their families.

Another legend tells of why bears walk on four legs, not on two like they originally did. A granddaughter of a great Modoc chief living near Mount Shasta walked over to a nearby river to wash herself. As she walked into the river, the waters swept her far downstream. A bear saw her plight, jumped into the river to save her, then took her with him to its home to feed her. Bears at that time walked on two legs, as we humans do now. The bear watched over her for a long time, and fell in love with her.

She became pregnant, and delivered a boy child that looked like her, with black hair as black as coal. Her grandfather had begun searching for her, and finally found her in the bear's home. Seeing that the boy looked nothing like him, he told the bear, "Get down on all four feet. You have dishonored me by becoming father to my grandson. From now on, all bears will be forced to walk on all four legs, never again to dishonor the human people."

A long time ago, all crows were white. Crows were friends of the buffalos, and would warn the buffalo when the Indian hunters would get close to the herd. The buffalos would run off, and the hunters would not be able to catch them. Selecting a smart young Pawnee boy, the hunters covered his body with a large buffalo robe. He then crawled up into the midst of a buffalo herd, and watched the crow alert the buffalos of the closeness of the hunting party. After finding out that the crow was responsible for their unsuccessful buffalo hunts, they caught the crow, and meant to teach it a lesson. They tied it up suspending it atop the smoke hole in their teepee, they started a fire below, turning the crow's body and feathers black. And that is why all crows are completely black in color.

There is another legend of a time when the Pawnee people who lived in the area where the state of Kansas is located today were starving, and no buffalos were in the territory near them. There was a young boy who lived with his grandmother who lived from the scraps of other families living nearby. He told her that he would find food for them by going out on his own into the vast valley next to the one where they were living.

He left one day and walked for several days before he fell over from exhaustion. He had a dream that a large buffalo came to him and said, "Two days from now, from the face of the mountain you can see ahead of you, there will be two buffalos coming from within the mountain whenever you clap your hands twice." The boy woke up from his dream, waited two days, and then approached the mountain before clapping his hands twice.

After the second clap, a hole opened up and two buffalos came charging out stopping in front of the boy. He returned to his village with the two buffalos following him, where the two buffalo were killed, stripped of their hides, and eaten. The people of his village were thrilled to see the buffalo, and the boy encouraged them to follow him to the next valley where he clapped his hands again twice and two more buffalos emerged from the hole that opened up. The young man went to this mountain each full moon thereafter, bringing forth the two buffalos each time until his grandmother died, when he left the village and never returned.

Many petroglyphs and pictographs portray the people dancing, the animals which the people hunted, and sometimes they depict the forms of scary creatures, or figures of people or animals that may have visited the locations from other worlds beyond our own. Winged serpents, or haloed figure heads, and even saucer-like figures were scratched into or painted on boulders. These petroglyphs and pictographs were the artist's attempt to illustrate their lives, or possibly what was going on inside their thoughts. It was, as our artists of today say, "expressing themselves."

Petroglyphs and pictographs are found all over the world. Some were found in Canada, Egypt, caves of France, South America and throughout the United States. These definitely try to tell the stories these people of long ago were trying to tell future peoples about their lives.

What would these people tell us about their lives if they could talk with us now? I am sure that first and foremost, they would emphasize our misuse and neglect of our and their mother earth.

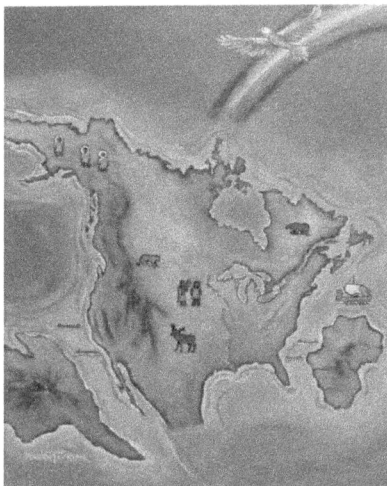

Chapter 5—Not One, but Many Nations

THE GREAT SIOUX Nation is composed of three dialects of a language, three branches of their heritage, and three locations in which they now live. The Lakota Nation is the largest, the Dakota the next in size, and the Nakota the smallest of the three. The three branches live in North and South Dakota, and Minnesota. However, their creation story is similar.

When the Great Mystery, named Wakan Tanka, became bored living alone in his home in the sky, he decided to shovel away the snow and ice from the floor on which his home was built. He shoveled until an open spot appeared, and began dumping the snow and ice through the hole until the hill of ice and snow below reached a height just below the level of the sky on which he lived. He lowered himself through the hole and began walking down the mountain of ice and snow.

As his footsteps were heavy, they reached below the ice and trees began growing from the bare ground where his huge footsteps had been. The beauty of the earth began blossoming, and he decided to bring his family down to live on the earth with him. Initially, the family lived within the hill of ice and snow. As they required heat and light, fires were built inside the hill, with sparks and clouds of steam rushing up through the open top. Then, the whole mountain would tremble. The wind would rush violently around and above the mountain, allowing the cold to come down through the hole and causing the family to become uncomfortably cold.

Feeling the need for more warmth, Wakan Tanka asked his youngest daughter to climb up the inside of the mountain and ask the wind to blow at a lesser speed. She was told not to peek above the rim of the hole as the wind could grasp her beautiful red hair and blow her away from their home. According to legend, she had heard that the oceans could be seen from the rim, so she peeked over the rim, and was promptly picked up by her hair, and blown far away. An eagle took pity on her, allowed her to reach up and hold onto one of its legs, and she was taken up to live with the eagle's family high on another mountain peak.

The young girl married the oldest of the eagle's offspring and the two had many children. When told of the location of the daughter, Wakan Tanka went to find her, and upon seeing that she had grown into a woman with offspring that did not look like her or himself, he left them, and the woman's children became the first Sioux Indians. As the children left the eagle's nest they found that they needed food and shelter, so they began hunting and gathering, digging pit houses for shelter, and having children of their own.

Switching to the Sioux nations, there is a legend of the Great Spirit scaring the entire tribe of the Dakota people at one time. As a storm approached the village below the great mountain, thunder and lightning had wakened the entire village one late evening. The scared people ran over to the lodge of the shaman, asking what they could do to appease the Great Spirit. He began to tell them the story of when the Great Spirit became angry with the red men living next to another large mountain. The Great Spirit began to vomit fire and hot stones high into the air, with all of that falling on the village, to terrify them. Their lodges, their families, and possessions were destroyed. After a time, the Great Spirit felt sorry for the Dakotas, put out the fire, and chased the storm away.

The reason for the Great Spirit becoming angry with the people is that he saw that they were badly misbehaving, and wanted them to return to the red way of living. The legend that the shaman told them took such a long time that the storm was long gone by the time he finished telling it. The people of that village had learned their lesson from the legend and returned to the red way of living.

According to the beliefs of the Dakota, Lakota, Nakota and Sioux, Wakan Tanka, symbolized by a sacred tree in the middle of their ceremonial Sun Dance, is at the center of the universe. The Sun Dance tree holds a nest at the point where the branches fork at the top. The nest is symbolized with cherry branches, and represents the nest of the thunder beings.

These people believe in a creator called Inyan, who was first. He created a companion who was called Wakinyan. Inyan began by bringing into being Maka, the earth. Secondly, he created Mini, the water, then Mahpiyato, the sky. At that point, Inyan had used all of his powers, shriveling up and becoming a rock. Maka, the earth began complaining about feeling cold, so that Mahpiyato said, "I will warm you," and the sky created the sun, the wind, the moon, and female buffalos, who lived underground. Now there was night, day, wind, water, but still no life above ground. Wakinyan said, "Let me create life." Wakinyan's voice is the thunder, the blink of his eye the flash of lightning.

With a bolt of lightning, he created fish and swimmers, all green vegetation, the birds of the air, and all four-legged animals. There was now life, but still no humans. There were only spirits on the earth at that time. The female buffalos had offspring, some of whom were human, and they sought a place above ground to live. They climbed out of a spiral cavern allegedly within the Black Hills of the Dakotas and became the Lakota people, who now live in North Dakota. The buffalos followed, becoming the foods which the humans ate, and whose hides protected many bodies and teepees until the 1880's when the buffalo nearly became extinct because of overkill by the white man's greed.

The Sun Dance is a very important religious ceremony of the Dakota Sioux. It takes place at a place called Sun Dance Mountain in the northwest corner of the Black Hills of South Dakota. The legend behind the dance is that a beautiful daughter of the chief was being courted by many of the well-known young braves of the tribe, but her heart was stuck on another young man who was poor, and not as well thought of. The poor boy went to the chief and asked him for his daughter to become his wife, but the chief said no.

The poor boy went to the shaman and asked what he should do in order to win the girl's hand, as she had already expressed her love for him. The shaman told him that if he were to get the sun god's approval and blessing, the chief would allow the marriage, and the entire tribe would benefit. The young man went looking for the sun god, walking many days to the east hoping to find the sun god's home. His provisions were few, and he ran out of food and water after many days of walking. He fell down from hunger and thirst along the path, and the sun god stopped along his flight across the sky, waking the young man and asking what he could do to help.

After being told that the young man needed his approval and blessing, the sun god gave the young man a special stone that shone a very bright light when angled toward the sun, and sent him back to his tribe with food and water. Upon reaching the tribe, the young man showed the stone to the chief, who called to a meeting all of the young men of the tribe who had been suitors for his daughter. He had the young man show the stone to the assembled people and received the approval of the chief. The following evening the young man and the daughter were married by the shaman, and there was a celebration which ended with the first Sun Dance. It is still performed annually, and is the most important celebration of the year.

One of the legends telling of the founding and eventual use of the peyote plant as a religious object in the Brule Sioux tribe of the Dakotas is that an old woman and her granddaughter lived in a village in which there were many sick people who were dying from an illness. The old woman was praying that she and her granddaughter would not be infected by the sickness that the other villagers were afflicted by.

During a dream catcher she had one night, she was told by a spirit that she was to search for an herb that, when used properly, would cure those that had the sickness and prevent others from getting the illness. The next morning, she and her granddaughter left the village on a vision quest before any other villagers had awakened. She and her granddaughter walked far into the woods near their home, and entered the long, hot desert looking for the herb she had seen during the dream catcher.

Arriving at the top of a hill just before the sun went down on the third day, she set about arranging a sleeping area surrounded by a few sticks she found in the area. The circle was made to keep snakes from entering and biting her and her granddaughter. Without food and water, the two huddled together, not knowing what to do. Just then, a huge bird, an eagle, passed above them, and the grandmother prayed to the eagle for wisdom and power. The next morning as they awakened, they saw the figure of a man floating in the air a few feet above them.

The man spoke saying, "You want food and water and do not know where to find it. I have a medicine for you. It will help you." The man's hand pointed toward a spot on the ground about four feet in front of the pair. There was a plant, known as peyote, growing there, a large plant that had sixteen green leaves extending from the top. She did not know what the plant was for, but she took her bone knife and cut off one of the leaves. She found moisture in the stem and she and her granddaughter drank some of the peyote juice, the water of life.

As they drank it, they were refreshed. Both of them ate some of the leaf and stem, and knowledge and understanding began flowing through their bodies. Although they had been lost, not remembering in what direction the village was located, they found the village on the second day, and began giving some of the peyote juice to the sickened people. Gradually the villagers regained their health and peyote became the largest part of their religious ceremonies. Besides drinking the peyote juice, other people smoke the peyote leaves in their pipes. This is a hallucinatory drug that is outlawed in many areas of the United States, but is used extensively by the Native American church in their ceremonies called Peyotism or the Peyote church.

Long, long ago, two young boys of the Lakota tribe were playing with a stone they kept throwing toward targets they kept changing, going farther and farther outside of their village. Then, they heard the sound of a small animal, and they began searching for it, the trail leading farther from the village. They found a small stream from which they drank some water, and seeing some pretty stones beneath the water, they began picking up the stones from the water leading them farther from their village. As the sun began to move far to the west, they decided to return to their home in the village.

However, they had lost their way, and did not know where the village was located. As it became dark, they laid down next to a large tree and went to sleep. Several times during the night an owl hooted, which was a bad omen to their people. In the morning, after waking up they were hungry, but did not know which berries, leaves or mushrooms would be good for them. They heard a loud crackling noise and turning around they saw a giant bear. They began running but the bear could run faster. They began to pray to the Great Spirit as the bear had almost caught them. As the prayers reached the Great Spirit, the boys began to run upwards toward the very high rock that seemed to grow with every step they took.

Up, up, up they ran, and as it almost reached the sky, they looked backward to see where the bear was. The rock was so high and the sides were so smooth that the bear could not climb it. The bear tried to climb the rock, leaving large lines in the rock where its' claws left marks, but the bear, although trying for any way of reaching the two boys by clawing at all sides of the rock could not reach them. The bear finally gave up walking away in defeat. An eagle saw the boys at the top of the rock and allowed them to grab onto its legs, and flew them back to their village.

Along with the people who entered North America via the Bering Land Bridge, there were others who entered through Iceland, Newfoundland, and Nova Scotia from the Scandinavian countries of Norway, Denmark and Sweden. That is why there are some indigenous people with blue eyes, and/or blond hair. Some historians say that Eric the Red and his son Leif Erikson were the first people to have navigated from Norway to Iceland, Newfoundland, and eventually to the Boston Harbor leading to the Charles River.

In fact, there is a statue of Leif Erikson on Commonwealth Avenue in Boston, Massachusetts recognizing his possible landing there in approximately the year 1000 AD, almost 500 years before Christopher Columbus arrived in the Bahamas Islands. In fact, Columbus never set foot in the Americas. It is certain however, that Eric and Leif did land in Iceland (where Leif Erikson was born in approximately 980 AD, and he and his father did land in Newfoundland where they set up a village before returning to Norway. It was from Newfoundland that Leif (nicknamed "Lucky") Erikson would have sailed south into the Boston Harbor in the year 1000 AD.

In my previous book, *When the Spirits Move*, I mentioned that I had been told by a Native American storyteller that there were three Native American hunters hunting near the Atlantic coastline near Boston who met a large white man with a long white beard. Through sign language, the white man had invited two of the hunters out to his ship, and then sailed off with them aboard. It might have been Leif Erikson they met. The hunters never returned to their clan after that. The hunters thought that the ship was the sun god's home as it had come from the east. The third hunter went back to his clan and told the people there that the two men had gone with the big white man to the sun god's home, and the sun god's home sailed away back east, from where it had come.

As some of the people who had made their way across what is

now Canada, these few Scandinavian people met with the arrivals from the west, forming small family villages. They moved often, following the food chain, as did the people who approached from the west. This led to misunderstandings because of language differences, jealousy and protection of prior hunting areas, and the need to protect and feed their families.

Particularly fierce were the wars between the Cree people approaching from the west and the Iroquois from the east. Each of these two groups encroached on the others' hunting grounds, often resulting in warfare. As groups grew through births and friendships with other groups, the warfare became more territorial, stretching over more of what was to become Canada, and down into what is now the central United States of America. The Iroquois nation solidified by joining with other groups and calling themselves the Iroquois confederation of five, and later six, tribes united under one alliance.

These groups, consisting of the Cayuga, Mohawk, Oneida, Onondaga, and Seneca, lived from the Hudson Bay area, along the northern tier of the Great Lakes, and eastward toward the Atlantic Ocean coast. A sixth group was added in 1722 when the Tuscarora joined the confederation. There were other groups that remained singular such as the Abnaki, Malecite, Micmac, Passamaquoddy, Penobscot, etc., living adjacent to the Atlantic coastlines of Eastern North America. Those people were agriculturists, as well as hunters, gatherers, and fishermen. All lived for the betterment of their families, clans, and later, tribes.

Languages and their origin is so important to try to put the various groups of people together. For an example, the Algonquian language used by the Algonquin, Arapaho, Blackfoot, Cherokee, Cree, Iroquois, Menomonee, Mi'kmaq, Mohawk, Ojibwa and many other tribes of Canada and the United States link some of them together. However, there were multiple dialects that were used by even those people.

Other than the Cree, these people seem to have entered North America from Atlantis and Europe, occupying the eastern parts of both Canada and the United States, and then expanded toward the west. From archaeological findings and teachings of the Mormon faith, Atlantis and European people entered North America about the same time as those that crossed the Bering land bridge, and became part of the groups whom the white men found as Amerindians.

Whether those Amerindians were parts of the Hopi, Acoma, Zuni, and other people who migrated toward the east (and whom I wrote about in my previous book, "When the Spirits Move") or whether they were from the earliest arrivals from the Bering land bridge is anybody's guess, as we were not there. However, many of the locations' names along the eastern half of Canada were taken from the French and Portuguese languages, leading one to believe they came from a different direction and background. The Hopi, Acoma, Pima and Tohono O'odham spoke the Uto-Aztecan language of the southwestern US and Central America. The Athabaskan language has been talked about enough in the preceding chapters.

The Algonquin creation story begins with two worlds, an upper and a lower world. The upper world was inhabited by animals, plants and people, while the lower was a water world, inhabited by birds, fish, and sea creatures who had no need for land. A young pregnant woman, who became known as Sky Woman, encouraged her husband to dig a hole around a very special tree which was known to be the Tree of Life so that she could look down on the lower world. As she stretched over to see the lower world, she lost her balance and fell toward the water world below.

A covey of geese saw her falling and flew below her holding her above the water until they found a very large turtle swimming below, dropping her slowly onto its back. Knowing that the turtle's back was uncomfortable for the woman to sit on, a number of sea creatures dove beneath the water and brought mud clutched in their claws from the bottom of the ocean up to place on the turtle's back to cushion the seat for the woman. The mud grew wider and stretched for a long distance. That is the reason that many of their

93

people consider North America to be known as Turtle Island.

Time came for Sky Woman to birth the child within her, and she birthed a daughter who grew very swiftly, and who was married and impregnated by the West Wind. During pregnancy, there were twin boys growing within the daughter, and between them, they decided that the first son was to be delivered the usual way, while the second burst out from under his mother's arm killing his mother. She was buried in the land covering the turtle's back, and from that land beans, berries, corn and squash grew for food; and tobacco grew for smoking to appease the spirit world living above.

The first son created the beautiful trees, grass, flowers, and the lakes, rivers and streams that provided the moisture for their growth. The second twin added thorns to cacti and bushes, such as the rose bush. He agitated the winds to create tornadoes, thunder and lightning to scare children, and water to overflow the banks of bodies of water. It was the second twin who sought out the methods by which he could kill the first twin, but it was the first twin that was able to discover the underhanded ways in which his brother was trying to kill him. Eventually, the first twin killed the second twin, but not until the elements were given the power to create the hardships on the generations of people that followed them.

The Algonquin creation story above is very unusual, as most of the creation stories of the indigenous people begin in dark worlds beneath the earth, and gradually enter the above worlds through a process of three worlds below the earth until emerging into the fourth world, the world in which we now live. However, the turtle becomes the basis of the earth in many, many of their legends and myths. Turtle Island is the basis for many of the creation stories.

As the people arrived on the islands to the east of North Carolina, they saw many wide sandy beaches, grass and beautiful tall trees, high hills in the background, and the many food sources they had missed while they were on board the ships that carried them from the faraway places they had left. Imagine the wonder they felt seeing whitetail deer, bobcats, black bears, coyotes, foxes, turkeys and other animals they had never seen before, coming from Atlantis or the desert lands of Egypt, Iran, Iraq, and Israel. They had never seen such large animals, other than the camels they had seen back in the Mediterranean areas.

They saw many different types of trees, and many lakes and streams leading to other areas of what they considered to be paradise. Fashioning wooden spears from straight branches, knapping stone for knives and axes, using the long grasses or strips of hides to tie the axe heads to forked branches, and utilizing all of the other available materials, they made tools and weapons with which to hunt, build shelters and protect themselves.

The large seashells could be used as shovels, the grasses woven into clothing, mats, and rope. Yes, all of these items were new to these people who had left their land in search of a better life for themselves and their families. They had to learn how to deal with the animals, bushes, and trees that they had never encountered before. The alligators, birds, fish, and snakes were new to them too. The people dug pit houses for shelter, cut tree branches to place over the pit openings for roofs, mixed mud to seal holes between the branches to keep the animals, wind, and rain out of their new homes.

During certain times of the year storms rolled in from the ocean, and tore their meager lives apart as the water rushed into their dugouts. Most of the people left the beaches and found refuge in the mountains, but that presented new issues. Their lives were all about learning, and learn they must in order to survive. Their beliefs were strong, but as time went on, their beliefs changed to the realities of their present situations.

The only areas that have not been covered are the southeastern United States and the Gulf states. From all indications I have found in the books I have read, the Seminole, Muscogee Creek, Natchez, and those bands and tribes from that area claim that they are Native Americans, which no books I have found, nor people with whom I have talked, dispute. Each of those tribes have lived in that area since before the 1500's when the Spanish arrived. The Seminole used the Muscogee language, but considered it their own. There were five tribes that banded together under the Creek Confederacy because of defensive concerns, but because of many smaller bands joining and dropping out, this confederacy was not very meaningful.

A legend of the Muscogee is another of how fire was brought to the people. A long, long time ago, the Muscogee people had no fire. When the weather turned cold they were very uncomfortable. The only fire was the fire that burned in an old tree on an island that was occupied by the weasels. The island was some distance from the Muscogee village, and since the water between the village and the island was quite deep, none of the Muscogee people wanted to try to steal it from the weasels.

Finally, a rabbit said that it would try to steal it and bring it to the village. The rabbit was known to be a great dancer, and the weasels celebrated certain times of the year with big dances. Before swimming over to the weasel's island, the rabbit rubbed a lot of pine tar on his head making the hair on his head stand straight up.

Then he swam over to the weasel's island when he saw them begin their dancing. He was welcomed by the weasels as his reputation as a great dancer had preceded him. He was even asked to lead the dancers as they danced nearer to the fire. As he got near enough to bow his head and ignite the hair on his head, he dashed back to the water and swam across before the weasels could catch him. The weasels asked the great Thunderbird to rain on the Muscogee village trying to snuff out the flame, but the rabbit had hidden the branch that he had set afire inside a hollow tree and the flame did not go out. The hair on his head was doused by the rain, and that is how the Muscogee village got fire.

Another of the Muscogee legends is that of the man and his dogs. The man was married to a wife who made him ill by giving him bad mushrooms to eat, and then fed him less food that would have returned him to health. It got so bad that he stayed in bed all the time, and his wife would beat his dogs every evening. Finally, the dogs asked the man if they could leave, but would not leave unless he would accompany them. He told the dogs he was too weak to get up, so the dogs picked up the bed and took it down to the fast-flowing water in the brook near the wigwam. They brought his bow and arrows with them, and as they floated downstream, stopping each night, and giving the man more food to eat, he got healthier. The dogs also told the man that his wife had another man hidden in a small home in the middle of the cornfield, and that they would go back and kill the man. They did go back and kill the man, returning to their master with blood on their faces.

As days went by, the man was able to rise and walk for a short while. The dogs encouraged the man to go hunting, and they flushed a big bear for the man to shoot and he killed the bear. After skinning the animal, the man packaged the meat and dried out the bear's hide, packing both in the boat. They returned upstream, stopping at another family's home for an evening. The family was quite old, but they had a young daughter, who was their only source for hunting and fishing for food. The man brought some of the bear meat to that family, and they all enjoyed a great meal prepared by the daughter. The family asked the man and his dogs to stay with them and help the daughter in hunting, and he married the daughter. He and the dogs stayed with the old family for as long as the old couple lived.

The southeastern part of the U.S. is subject to great storms called hurricanes that sweep in from the Atlantic Ocean with extremely high winds and so much rain it floods many low-lying areas. These storms would destroy the homes of the people who lived there even though some lived on hilltops.

The hurricanes would last for several days during which the people would seek out shelter anywhere they could find it. The safest places were caves, but they were not to be found in all of the places the people lived. The people's world was turned upside down during these terrible storms, and it would take many days to try to rebuild their homes and lives. Some of the people traveled west into what is now Alabama and Mississippi, but the hurricanes followed them, no matter where they went.

During these storms their prayers were thought to be hopeless, as the eagles who were to take the prayers to the Great Spirit were nowhere to be seen, nor heard. There were rare occurrences when the winds would become very cold and even snow blew into the areas in which these people lived in what is now northern Florida and Georgia. The return to blue skies and brilliant sunshine were welcomed with ceremonial dances being performed soon after their appearances.

Life was not easy for these people. Moving constantly meant digging pit houses, cutting branches and scraping mud with which to patch and cover the roofs of the pit houses, collecting and growing food at one location while following the animals that provided meat, fishing the waters for fish, turtles, or other foods that became more available. Alligators and snakes were very common in the southeastern parts of the U.S. Knowing how to cope with those types of animals was a real learning experience. Finding adequate shelter from rain, snow, hail or wind storms was essential, whether it be spring, summer, fall or winter. Clothing was provided by animals' skins, bark from trees, feathers from birds, and grasses or moss growing from the ground. Mother Earth provided everything needed for them to care for themselves and their families, but it was their responsibility to find them and use them responsibly. Almost everything they learned were through trial and error.

The entry of the Cherokee nation is one of the most intriguing stories of all. The lost city of Atlantis, which was supposedly an island located between Europe and North America, has been a possible origin for those people. Is it possible that as the Atlantic Ocean began covering that island, the people chose either an eastern or western route to leave it? The written language could have been taken to Egypt, Iran, Iraq, Israel, and Portugal by traveling eastward, or to North America by sailing westward. That is an explanation for the paintings and scratchings (pictographs and petroglyphs) on rocks, from the eastern shores of North America to the state of Minnesota, of a supposedly written language that relates to the Mediterranean areas.

A doctor, Donald Yates, a member of the Cherokee Nation, who has done much work researching DNA of the Cherokee nation, hypothesizes that a group of Ptolemaic followers from either Atlantis or Egypt, Iraq, Iran, and Israel sailed to the shores of North America approximately during the 300 B.C. time period, ostensibly arriving on the shores of North Carolina, and established roots there to become the Cherokee Nation.

They became one of the fiercest tribes in all of North America. Many from that group continued searching for the perfect home sites in the Smoky Mountain area of what is now the United States. However, many people of that area were gathered together by the government of the United States and forced to travel westward beyond the Mississippi River on what has been called "the trail of tears" during the 1830's, and were given land by the United States government in northeastern Oklahoma. Others of the Cherokee nation hid out in the Smoky Mountains of North Carolina, were not found, did not participate in that long walk, and remain there today.

There have been many stories detailing rock art that resembles the writing of old Latin, French, and Portuguese languages found on rocks from Minnesota to Maine and south to the Carolinas. It is reasonable to assume that there were visitors from other countries before Christopher Columbus found the new world of the Bahamas in 1492, which he mistakenly called India and its occupants, Indians.

And it wasn't until 1504 when Cortez left Spain to find riches and souls for the Catholic Church and the king of Spain that the shores of Cuba and later Mexico were breached, conquered, and recorded. The Latin, French and Portuguese languages were not spoken by indigenous people Cortez found upon entering these lands, and yet, there are many locations that have names that refer to those languages.

The French imprinted their culture throughout the eastern half of Canada and the Spanish influence has carried over throughout the United States, Mexico, Central and South America. The British arrived in 1607, and the rest of the European continent followed. France entered the areas which became Alabama, Louisiana, and Mississippi, and Russia entered from the west. North America had become the melting pot of the world. Since there were no known written languages at the time of their arrival, the Native American and indigenous people used figures of animals, objects of nature, and likenesses of people when carving or painting into or onto stone walls. Such likenesses were carved or painted onto walls all over the world long before those that are found in North America.

New foods, such as mushrooms, nuts, and berries had to be tasted and checked to be sure they were digestible and not poison to their bodies and minds. New methods of hunting and gathering arose as trees gave them both assistance—they could hide behind them as they approached their prey—but also a detriment, as there were no clear straight shots over a distance while in a wooded area. The trees also furnished the fuel, shelters, and weapons they needed during their everyday lives. The leaves and small branches helped start and fuel the fires, the larger branches provided the walls and ceilings for their shelters, and the straight, thin branches were fashioned into bows, arrows and spears, while the notched branches became the handles of axes, hatchets, and knives. Everything that the Great Spirit provided them had a use, and nothing was to be wasted.

Legends and myths are stories told by the elders or storytellers to members of their clans to which they belong. They are told to direct, entertain, explain, and inform members of their history and the reasons their lives are impacted by different happenings. The most important circumstances involve ancestors, animals, and/or, the weather and its various parts—sun, rain, wind, hail, snow, and ice. The ancestors were usually honored by the tales of their deeds.

Animals could be as small as ants and spiders, or as large as whales, and could be helpful or harmful to the people of long ago when stories are told about them. Giants, monsters and tiny people were part of the legends and myths too. The sun brings needed light and heat, the rains bring moisture. The winds conduct air circulation, while hail, snow and ice produce cold and running water. Each was important to all life forms.

The sun was essential for growth, the rain supplied the water that is necessary for life to survive, with the wind furnishing the air all life forms need to live. Finally, hail, snow, and ice, during and after melting, allow water to enter the ground as well as move through brooks, lakes, oceans, rivers, and streams. This cleanses the earth from the impurities left behind by the dying off of leaves from bushes, flowers, and trees, as well as wastes left behind by animals, fires, and people. Legends and myths about ancestors are very important as they inform the listeners of who they are in relation to those people of long ago. There is great honor bestowed on those ancestors who have gone before in the stories told by the elders and storytellers.

Also, animals, birds, fish, sun, moon, stars, and the plants and trees each are honored by the stories told about them. As you have read before in this book and others I have written, the turtle is one of the most revered, as it carries the world and the calendar on its back. The coyote is regarded as a helper and a trickster to people, as are many of the animals. The eagle is often portrayed as the go-between for the people's prayers and the Great Spirit. The rabbit was very important to the legends and myths of the people of the northeast. When we hear these stories, we hear of the history of this land and its people, the things that surround and influence our and their lives, with a large dose of instruction on how to treat other people and things in nature.

A legend of the great Yellowstone Valley in what is now known as Yellowstone National park in the states of Montana, Idaho, and Wyoming was one of the places in which the Cheyenne people took refuge during the great flood. It is said as the rain came down, and the water line rose, the Cheyenne people looked for a place where the water would not reach them.

They climbed the hills around the places where they lived, but the water line approached the tops of the hills. They went to mountains where they thought they would be safe. Finally, they decided to ask the old medicine man, Spotted Bear, what they could do to save themselves. He told them that the Great Spirit told him that the only way to save themselves was to find a white buffalo, and from that time on they would be told what to do. Two young hunters went out and found a buffalo family, a cow and calf standing next to a dead white buffalo bull. They quickly stripped the hide from the dead white buffalo bull and took the hide back to Spotted Bear. After praying above the hide which laid on the ground in front of where he sat, he began smoking his peace pipe and surrendering his mind to the spirit world. After a short while, he asked five men to take hold of corners of the white buffalo hide, beginning to stretch it as the rain fell upon it.

As with all hides, it stretched as the rain fell and they got help from other men to continue stretching the hide over the entire village and beyond. As it was stretched, no rain fell on the village as the hide acted as a roof for the village. It continued to stretch until one end was attached to the top of Bridger Mountain in the west, another to the Pryor Mountains. The other ends were attached to the Bear Tooth and Crazy Mountains, and the last end to Signal Butte in the Bull Mountains. Still the rains fell and the huge hide sagged from all of the weight. Spotted Bear walked up to the corner of the hide which had been fastened to the Bridger Mountain to the west, and, lifting up the corner, the west wind blew beneath the hide and began drying the land, and that allowed the birds, animals, and plant life to return to that part of their world.

Following the flood, the many people who had survived it began their searches for food and shelter, migrating north, south, east and west from where they emerged from hiding, or had been sheltered. They had to find areas that had dried out, and that meant slopes of mountains, high hills, or arid areas of deserts. It is understandable that sea shells are discovered all over the deserts of the southwest, but there came a time when mother earth dried out leaving the objects where they laid. These sea shells became jewelry, tools or utilities that adorned the bodies of people or were used to dig, scrape, and turn the sand or ground as new homes were built.

During that flood, in what is now eastern Arizona at a place called the Petrified National Forest, the trees became so water-logged that their roots were unable to hold them upright, and they fell over. The water was absorbed by the wood, and as they eventually dried out, the logs became petrified, or changed to stone. As you go through that area, you will see many colors in the rings of stone within the logs. It is a beautiful area to visit, right next to the Painted Desert. There was a river that wound its way through that area called the Puerco River, and right next to the dry banks was an old pueblo ruins by the name of the Puerco ruins.

It was at those ruins that my mother, father, my wife, Opal, and I were exploring one day in 1982 when a bus drove up and some of the people exited the bus and walked up to my father and told him they had witnessed his musical band play a concert in Milwaukee, Wisconsin a few weeks before.

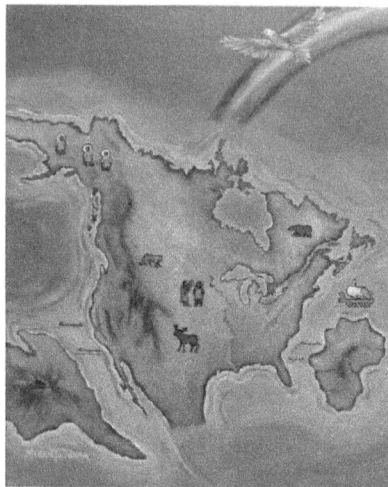

Chapter 6—The Search for Light and Warmth

THERE ARE MANY, many more legends and myths that tell of the needs and wants of these people who came to this continent for the same things our forefathers sought. What were those things each of them sought? There was peace, harmony with family and friends, food, clothing, and shelter, ability to gather or hunt (work) for the necessities of life, and religious freedom, and provide for their families. There may have been more, but these were at, or near, the top of what we all want for ourselves and our families.

One of the families, a father, mother and young boy child, lived alone and was faced with a shortage of food during the winter one year. The father went out hunting one early morning, and found buffalo tracks leading away from where he and his family lived. He followed the tracks until it began getting dark, and hurried home to be with the family overnight. As he approached his home, he heard his young son crying out that he was hungry and wanted something to eat. The man, hearing the son crying, turned around and began hunting in the dark, trying to find something, anything for his son to eat. A wolf heard his heavy breathing as he searched in the darkness, and asked the man what he was doing out so late at night. The man told him that his family was starving, and he needed to find food for them as quickly as possible.

He told the wolf he was trying to find the buffalo he had been tracking earlier that day. The wolf said, "I will help you. Take my bow and arrows and hide behind this tree. I will find the buffalo and run him back this way. Be sure to use my bow and arrows when you shoot the buffalo, not yours." Off the wolf ran, searching for the buffalo the man had been tracking. The man looked at the bow and arrows the wolf had given him, and saw that they were of an inferior wood than his own, but he remembered what the wolf had said.

After a while, there was a pounding noise coming through the woods, and a buffalo came charging right at the tree behind which the hunter stood. The hunter used the wolf's bow and arrows, shooting not one, but six buffalos that ran toward him. There was a seventh that came at him, but he decided he would use his own bow and arrows to shoot it. The seventh buffalo dodged the arrow and kept running.

The wolf came up to the hunter and asked why he hadn't gotten the seventh buffalo and when told that the man had used his own bow and arrow, the wolf said, "What had I told you? You were to use my bow and arrows. Our families are still hungry, so let's cut up this meat of the last buffalo and take it to them." They did cut up the sixth buffalo and divided the meat between them, taking the food to their respective families. The next morning the hunter and his family met the wolf and its family at the place the buffalos had been shot.

The two families cut up the meat of the five remaining buffalos, storing it for use later that winter. The wolf's pups and the young son of the hunter began playing together, and that is how wolf pups became domesticated dogs and man's best friends.

Symbolism is very important to the indigenous and Native American people, and they used symbols in everything they did.

Clothing, dolls, jewelry, paintings, petroglyphs, pictographs, pottery, rugs, and shelters were enriched with the symbols of their beliefs and heritage. I have a six feet by four feet woven rug in my living room which has a two horned shaman wearing a headdress of three feathers for healing, with rain signs falling from his hands and gown.

There is also one feather hanging down from each of the two horns. There is a circle of life in the middle of the rug, with eight arrows separating each of the four corn symbols to denote the spring (planting, or beginning of life) from twelve to three o'clock, and fall (harvest season) from six to nine o'clock, with the growing season from three to six o'clock and the dying season from nine to twelve completing the circle. There is a broken circle surrounding the circle of life, with the four symbols of the seasons breaking that circle.

On the right side there is another human figure, possibly another shaman with two feathers as a headdress, and from its left ear there is an extension to listen for words spoken by the Great Spirit. Its arms are extending downward, and it looks like it is carrying four four-pronged pitchforks with two eagle feathers dangling from each of the handles, and straight sticks that may have been used in making holes in which seeds were planted. The clothing worn by the two figures display a Kachina clan symbol above a butterfly symbol in the middle of both his/her gowns.

There are two filled-in white circles down the front of the gown of the figure on the left side. There were other smaller symbols shown on the gowns which I could not identify. Around the entire rug's symbols, there is a rectangular frame for the picture. It is interesting to note that every feather in this rug is an eagle feather rather than a turkey feather. This rug is one of the first items my wife and I purchased for our first home in Ahwatukee, Arizona in 1991.

I believe it might have been a Hopi weaver that wove that rug, but it may have been of Navajo design. This is the most treasured original Native American artifact I have in my possession. Some of the other artifacts we have in our condominium are a ten inch turtle rattle, a four-foot wooden spear with stone point and feathers on the handle, a small eight inch wooden ladder, and a buffalo bone knife decorated with feathers and a beaded handle.

Also, the original oil painting covers from each of my published books hang in the dining room, and a beautiful carved eagle embedded in a blue sky painted wooden background sits on one of the straight-backed chairs. We also have a carved wooden corn doll, several Kachina dolls, and other indigenous dolls throughout the unit. Each room in the condominium, including entranceway, bathrooms and bedrooms, have authentic dream catchers and/or spirit windows.

As the Apache bands migrated farther south and west they met with other groups of Native Americans and indigenous people who were more established in those areas. The Apache bands would search out the best locations for food, be it animals such as bears, beaver, deer, elk, quail and turkey, or the berry bushes, mushrooms, nut-bearing trees, or the fish, turtles or other edible swimming animals found in the lakes, rivers or streams.

They would fight for the right to use that area for as long as the food was available to them, or until they were defeated by a stronger force. Although there was ice, sleet, snow, and wind during the winters, the summers were very warm, or even hot. They adapted to the weather rather easily as it had been so much colder as they crossed the ice bridge and entered Alaska and Canada. Having survived the hand to mouth style of living for so long, they began to collect and save foods for later use, which helped them stabilize their diets and live more balanced lives.

The White Mountain band kept walking southward until they found the mountainous area east of the Phoenix, Arizona area now called the White Mountains. There they lived, hunted, and gathered, for many years until the white men entered the area, searching for gold and silver. They began fighting for what they considered their homeland, and way of life. The U.S. government built Fort Apache in the White Mountains, near Greer, AZ., and is one of the popular locations to experience the pow-wows that take place there periodically.

A great legend of the Apache bands is that of the thunderbird, whose home was said to be in the Superstition Mountains approximately forty miles east of Phoenix, Arizona. It was from that mountain range the thunder and lightning preceded the wind and rain that fell on the various camps of the Apache bands living to the east and south of that range.

That mountain range was sacred ground to them as rain meant moisture which furnished the water for the lakes, rivers and streams near to where they lived. During the hot summers they needed those waterways to flow freely for drinking, cooking, washing bodies, clothing and utensils. Their legends and myths led them to walk around that range rather than stepping on the holy ground. In fact, after a group of Mexican miners led by the Peralta family opened a mine by the name of the Sombrero mine in 1845, the Apache bands came together to massacre the entire group in 1848, after which they covered the mine, and supposedly no one has ever found the mine again.

It is also said that the Apache bands have stationed guards around the mine entrance, which are to keep anyone from ever reopening the mine. This led to the legendary Lost Dutchman's gold mine mystery that prevails people even now to search the Superstition Mountains looking for the gold he supposedly left behind. Many people have searched in vain to find the gold, and many unexplained curious deaths have occurred to those who went there to find it. Could it be that the guards who stand beside the entrance had anything to do with the curious deaths of those who seek the gold?

The Chiricahua band went beyond the White Mountain band into the southeastern part of Arizona into an area now called the Chiricahua Mountains. The land there is filled with spires, hills and mountains that hid them away from all people who sought them. I drove down there once looking for Cochise's hideout, for he is buried in a secret unmarked grave somewhere in that area. I drove down a small one-track road until I came to an area so narrow, I could not proceed any further ahead. I had to back out to an area where I could turn around and drive back out. While I was at the area at which I had to begin to back up, there was a white-tailed deer that came up to the driver's side window and looked into the car. This is the middle of nowhere, believe me. It was a wonderful feeling, knowing that I had entered an area where animals were not afraid of people, and people were able to see nature as the Great Spirit intended it to be.

The Yaqui band walked even further to the south and set-up their villages on the southeast Arizona and Mexico border, and now live in both countries. The community of Guadalupe, AZ, a suburb of Phoenix, is largely composed of members of the Yaqui band, who hold a performance of their very colorful and religious deer dance annually through the streets of the community. The procession-like event is held starting from the Our Lady of Guadalupe Catholic church and ends up on Main Street.

The participants wear the masks and horns of the deer and wear rattles around their ankles made from butterfly cocoons (honoring the insect world). Their steps are meant to resemble the deer they represent on a cadence from a water drum (the deer's heartbeat), rasp (the deer's breathing), the gourd rattles (honoring the plant world) held and rattled to the pulse of the drumbeats by the participants, and the many, many colorful and beautiful flowers (honoring the flower world).

It is a great honor to be a participant in this and other deer dances performed in the Yaqui villages, and the participants take great pride in becoming a costumed dancer. It was a great honor to be invited to watch the ceremony be performed back in 2007, or thereabouts.

The Hualapai, Yavapai and Havasupai are also of the Apache bands. They live in the bottom of the Grand Canyon, and have lived there for centuries. Living within one of the most visited National Parks, but in an area not many people visit, allows them to be practically unknown. The Hualapai nation name is "the people of the tall pines." They live along the southern shores of the Colorado River. The Yavapai nation is known as "the people of the sun", although at the bottom of the canyon there is limited sunlight peering from above. The Havasupai nation means "the blue-green water people." The beautiful waterfalls within the Grand Canyon, the Havasupai Falls, is what draws people to their land.

These three bands speak a variation of the Yuman language, also spoken by indigenous people living in the northern part of the Baja, California. These three bands were very peaceful people who chose to be agriculturists, hunters and gatherers rather than warriors. The Quechan Nation of western California are close relatives and speak the same language.

The last of the indigenous people who crossed the Bering land bridge into what is now Alaska, entering what is now the lower United States, and migrating to the southwest were the Navajo nation. Not quite as aggressive as the Apaches, but just as hungry, they gradually took over the huge territories the pueblo people had hunted, gathered, and lived in from supposedly the beginning of time.

As the Navajo arrived during the time of the most serious drought in the 1250-1300 AD timeframe, the pueblo people had already moved from the wide-open spaces to places near water, and places they could more easily defend. Caves, high hills around water sources and hidden places were important for the defensive-minded agriculturists, even though they still went on hunts and gathering events around a closer proximity to their new homes. The Navajo began taking over the prior homes of the Anasazi, Hohokam, and Salado pueblo people, ancestors of the Hopi, Acoma, Zuni, Pima and Tohono O'odham (Papago) tribes of modern times.

Two of the most revered of the Navajo deities were a woman called "She who Changeth" and her younger sister, "White Shell Woman." "She who Changeth" was made of blue turquois of the land, and "White Shell Woman" was made of the white shell of the ocean. Each of these sisters gave birth to a son, and the father of both was the sun god. As the two sons grew up as cousins, they were so close they were thought of as brothers. They often asked their mothers, "Who is our father?" The two mothers would never tell them until they became men.

The two mothers told the men that their father was the sun, and they made preparations to seek him out and ask for favors from him. They were told by the wind that their father lived far to the east, and they began walking in that direction. They walked for many moons, using the rainbow road provided for them by the wind. Finally, as they approached the great waters in the east, they saw the magnificent home in which their father lived with his wife and his two other sons, Black Thunder and Blue Thunder.

Their father put the two young men through a number of trials, which both of them passed easily. The father became proud of them, and asked them what they desired. They told him of the giants and ghosts that were threatening their clans in their village, and they asked for weapons with which to slay the evil ones. Their father gave them helmets, shirts, leggings, and moccasins, all made of black flint.

When they put this armor on, lightning flashed from their joints as they flexed their arms and began to walk around the room. For weapons, the sun gave each of his sons a magical stone knife and a magical bow with arrows of rainbow, sunbeams, and lightning. The two brother-cousins left their father's home in the east and after returning to their mothers' homes, slew the

Ones, and their mothers and the village held a ceremonial dance to honor the men. A short time later, their father visited the young men's mothers, asking them to prepare a great home for him in the west so that he would be able to rest after his long trip above mother earth each day.

Some of the most interesting locations which were taken over by the Navajo people were Canyon de Chelly (Canyon de Shay), Monument Valley on the Arizona/Utah border, and the entire area between their four sacred mountains, Mount Blanca to the east in New Mexico, Mount Taylor (the Turquois mountain) to the south in New Mexico, San Francisco mountain (the San Francisco peaks in

111

northern Arizona above Flagstaff to the west, and Hesperus Mountain to the north in Colorado. It was their belief that they would be safe if they stayed within those four mountains, and that is approximately where the U.S. government granted them the largest reservation in the United States.

In fact, the Navajo reservation is larger in size than the entire state of West Virginia, and is larger than four other states of the United States. Unfortunately, the US government forced the Navajo to suffer through a "long walk" from their homes in Arizona to the far reaches of eastern New Mexico, a place called Bosque Redondo, which took approximately eighteen days in 1864. In 1868, the Navajo Nation was given permission to return to their homes in Arizona, and the permanent reservation rights were given to them. The Navajo reservations covers parts of northeastern Arizona, northwestern New Mexico, southeastern Utah, and a very small section of southwestern Colorado.

There was a very poor Apache man, who had been outcast by his band. He began living outside a Hopi pueblo tribe's village near the mountains of eastern Arizona. He lived on the scraps they threw away. One day he went on a hike that took him near a cliff, below which lived an eagle's family.

After peering over the edge, he saw the nest below which contained several young eaglets. He lost his balance and fell down into the nest, and had no way of climbing back to the ledge. Realizing his plight, he began taking care of the eaglets, hoping that his good works would enable him to be befriended by the mother and father of the eaglets. As they returned to the nest, they saw that their eaglets had been taken care of by the Apache man, and decided that he could stay with them.

They opened the rock door next to the nest and invited him in. The mother and father eagles took off their eagle suits and became a man and woman, just as the Apache man. They all sat down at a table within the home in the rock, and some food was passed around to all of them. The Apache man thought to himself, "This little bit of food will not be enough for me," but after eating it, he was satisfied. The three talked among themselves for a short while, when there was a knock on the door. The mother opened the door to several eagles waiting outside, and their leader asked whether they would like to explore the mountains around their home for a while. The mother and father agreed, but asked whether the Apache man could accompany them.

The leader said that that would be okay, and they uncovered a spare suit of eagle clothes for the man. After putting on the eagle suit the man joined the eagles as they left the rock house, and the Apache man thought to himself, "How wonderful it is to fly above the trees, among the mountains, and over the village of the pueblo people I have left behind." Then, because of all of the effort it took to fly that far, he began to be very tired and was passed up by all of the eagles with whom he had been flying.

Seeing him losing altitude and the strength to continue flying on his own, the eagles returned to fly below him, and gently landed him on the ground near the village. Asking for the eagle suit to be returned, they allowed the man to rest a while, after which the eagles all flew off. The man returned to the place outside the village where he had lived, and was grateful and satisfied with what he could get to eat and drink from the scraps of the Hopi villagers.

Many Navajo people lived in the Canyon de Chelly (Shay) area of northeastern Arizona in the early 1860's. By direction of the US government, the army led by Kit Carson, were directed to round up all of the Navajo people and force them to march to Bosque Redondo in the eastern New Mexico territory. They were found to be living in the canyons that ran from Canyon de Chelly.

There were many Navajo women and children killed in Massacre Canyon by the army as they shot from the rim above at anything that moved down below. This happened during the winter of 1863-64. After the massacre, the Navajo people were rounded up and forced to walk 300 miles from the canyon to Bosque Redondo during the 18 day walk. In 1868 a treaty was signed, a reservation was assigned for the Navajo people and they walked back to the area from which they had been driven.

Interestingly, some of the legends and myths of the Apache and Navajo people are of death, and how it affects the families of those who have died. If death took place inside the homes of a family, after the body was removed, the home was destroyed, and anything belonging to the deceased is destroyed as well. The family either built a new home or moved to another home within the extended family.

Legend says that the spirit of the dead person travels to the west, and is then taken into the sky to the seven stars of the Pleiades in the constellation of Taurus the Bull, where its spirit is judged before allowing it to enter the alleged place of the "happy hunting grounds." It is believed that if the person did not live the "red life", or the good life, the spirit was sent back to earth as another form of life to try again.

Some of the lesser known legends are of interest such as the supposed tribe of Welsh origin. According to legend, these people were to have descended from a colony founded by prince Madoc of Wales in 1170 AD. In Welsh history, Madoc was one of the sons of Owain Gwynedd, a great but belligerent Welsh king. Upon his father's death, other sons began fighting over who was to be the successor to the throne.

As Madoc was weary of the bloodshed, he decided to sail west, where he reached an unknown land. He left 120 men as a colony and returned to Wales in order to pick up ten ships loaded with men, women and livestock and return to his colony. There is no record of Madoc after he and the ships left Wales. This time period was at least several hundred years before Christopher Columbus left Spain in 1492.

Some say that this legend was initiated in order for England to enter a claim of founding North America before Spain. The legend goes on to say that the Welsh colony was part of the Mandan culture in North Dakota, which might explain the blue eyes and blonde hair of some of the indigenous people found in North America. Again, no proof of that has ever been found. An added legend goes on to say that one of the Welshmen was captured by Native Americans.

Supposedly as he was being readied for execution, he began praying in his language and the Native American captors recognized his words as their own language and released him.

Other legends indicate indigenous people arriving in South America by boat from across the Pacific Ocean. According to some people, there have been sunken longboats found along the coast of South America that date back to around 750 AD when the Mayan culture was overrun by the Aztec culture. If that is true, then some of the Aztec DNA should indicate some Indonesian beginnings. The war-like Aztecs easily defeated the agriculturist Mayans, and brutally ruled Mexico and northern Guatemala until the arrival of the Spaniards in the 1500's. Much blood was spilled through human sacrifices during the Aztec's rule.

Wandering the great expanses of North America, the many clans of various bands of people found the light and warmth of daylight expanded as they walked south. Those that had walked eastward into the center and beyond of Canada found the huge Hudson Bay. Those walking southeastward found the Great Lakes region of what separated Canada from the United States. Others walked south along the rivers and streams that became or fed the Columbia and Snake Rivers of Washington and Oregon.

At one time, a long, long time ago, according to legends and myths of the indigenous people who live in that area, there was a bridge that connected Mount Hood in the state of Oregon and Mount Adams in the state of Washington over the Columbia River. The two mountains were constantly arguing which was better. Finally, the Great Spirit had heard enough. He split the bridge, and moved the two mountains further apart settling the argument forever. The rapids in that area of the Columbia River are the supposed remnants of the destroyed bridge.

There are many, many exciting and interesting places to see in my area of the great Southwest. My exploration of the states of Arizona, Nevada, New Mexico, and Utah have brought me great pleasure and a sense of understanding how pre-historic people lived, played and worked. Driving along highway 40 just west of

Albuquerque, New Mexico is a special place called Sky City Casino, owned by the Acoma Indian nation. They live twelve miles south of highway 40 on a mesa that is 400 feet above the valley floor. If you stop at the casino, ask for a tour of the mesa, and you won't be disappointed in what you learn. The hotel offers comfortable rooms at an inexpensive price, the casino play is decent, and the restaurant has special pricing every evening if you have a free player's club card. Most of the people working for the various parts of the business are Acoma people, cousins of the Hopi people.

As near as we can surmise, the Apache and Navajo people arrived in the southwestern United States between the 900 AD's and 1250 AD. Somewhere during the latter days of those times, the pueblo people who were the hunters, gatherers, and agriculturists began moving to places where water brought food in the form of thirsty animals, allowed the people to dig canals to water their agricultural fields, and provided good drinking water and a place to bathe and wash clothes, pots, and dishes.

The 1200's AD was a period of extreme drought, necessitating their movement to those important areas. The Gila, Salt, and Verde rivers were the most available waterways stretching from the east to the west in the land we call the state of Arizona. Unfortunately, these rivers did not offer much in the way of protection for villages, as much of the water flowed along level ground as it raced westward from the hills next to the Superstition Mountain east of what we call the Valley of the Sun.

The largest village in the area was called Snaketown, which had an estimated 25,000 residents at one time, and was located near the western edge of what is now Chandler, Arizona. The Pima (Hohokam) people were the residents of that village.

The Hopi (Anasazi) people moved to the northeastern part of Arizona, living primarily on the three mesas where they now live. The oldest continuously lived in village in North America was Oraibi, which was inhabited from the 1200's to 2013, when the last inhabitants gave up their homes that had no running water, toilets, and other modern conveniences, moving to the more modern(?)

homes on the three mesas occupied by their descendants, the Hopi Nation. Visiting their mesa homes is eye-opening, as you find their homes there quite primitive, compared to the homes in which we live. You are welcome to visit their mesas, but request a native guide so that their lifestyles can be explained to you. They do have a visitors' center, fine restaurant, and a museum which is very instructive and worthwhile.

Many of the sites of these people's villages are open to the public as city, county, national or state parks. Some of the most interesting are the Mesa Verde National park near Cortez, Colorado. It is the largest of the ancestral Puebloan people's parks with over 600 cliff dwellings. The cliff dwellings are among the most widely visited in the southwest, with my favorite being the Cliff Castle, the largest cliff dwelling in North America.

The kivas within the ruins are exquisite, and you can almost feel the power and strength coming from within as you pass by them. Just a warning for those who visit the Cliff Castle ruins, there is a ladder which must be climbed as you exit the ruins. There are many different villages within the park, and all of them are worth visiting for their beauty, historical significance, and locations. Park rangers take you on the trails to the various village sites from the park's huge visitors' center.

A unique area to explore in northern Arizona is Antelope Canyon, a slot canyon area which offers unbelievable picture opportunities of the vertical slots within the sandy walking areas. This area is near Page, Arizona and the Glen Canyon Dam, and guides are always helpful.

Another of the unique Anasazi locations is Chaco Canyon north of Grants, New Mexico. Because it is about 40 miles north of highway 40, it does not get as many visitors, but it is one of the most sacred places for the Native American people, as it was the location that brought many thousands of people there to gather, pray, and trade. There is a very unusual stand of boulders which, at noon on the solstice (June 21st) each year, has a sharply pointed rock that points to the exact middle of a circle on another boulder. As we might understand it, it is the time of the year that changes from the longest amount of sunlight that day to lesser amounts as the days pass by to December 21st, the shortest day of sunlight each year. As the Hopi say, "That is the time the sun god turns around."

Monument Valley is an unforgettable place to visit as it is on the border of Utah and Arizona, and the place where John Ford produced so many western pictures with John Wayne as the main star. Seeing the left and right mittens right before your eyes replaces the scenes you remember from the movies you have watched over and over again at home or in the theaters. The only thing that is missing is John Wayne himself. You can stay at the Goulding Lodge where many of the actors stayed, or the newer View hotel run by the Navajo nation. Both offer objects that the Native American or indigenous people have crafted such as woven blankets, jewelry, rugs, and other remembrances.

The Grand Canyon of the Colorado River is the national park that many tourists come to see at least once during their lifetimes. It is the most popular of the national parks of the southwestern United States, and the views from both the south and north rims are stunning. You see the Colorado river way down below, with the water rushing through narrows and bending within the steep canyon walls, holes in the walls that bring to mind the people of so long ago who lived in those caves.

Some adventuresome people may decide to take the raft tours through the canyon, visit the villages of the Hualapai and Yavapai bands at the bottom of the canyon. Helicopters and jeeps take tourists to those places, or the hale and hardy may hike down, but please remember, it is a two-way hike and going down is a lot easier than returning to the top. Many tours start from Las Vegas, Nevada, Williams, Arizona, or Sedona, Arizona, all serviced by busses, planes, or the Grand Canyon train from Williams, Arizona.

Canyon de Chelly (Canyon de Shay) is a huge canyon which contains many interesting views of places that were important to history. As you look down into the canyon from the rim above, you see sheep, goats, and cattle, tended by men or boys walking or on horseback, and the fields of beans, corn and squash being grown. Off in the distance you can see the White House ruins, a village stuck into the cliff several hundred yards from where you are standing, and a trail leading down into the canyon toward the ruins.

Yes, it is all there for you to see, and if you want to explore the interior, there are many tour guides available at the visitors' center. Spider Rock, the supposed home of spider woman, rises 800 feet as a needle toward the rim that encircles the canyon. It is said that spider woman watches for Navajo children misbehaving, and during the night, steals them from their homes and takes them up to her home, never to be seen again. Also, massacre canyon, where the army, led by Kit Carson, killed Navajo women and children before they were captured along with any remaining men and made to march to Oklahoma on their "long walk." This location is near Chinle in the northeastern part of Arizona.

Another amazing Anasazi location is Walnut Canyon national monument, a few miles east of Flagstaff, Arizona off of highway 40. It is what I would describe as an island in the sky, however there is a walkway from the visitors' center to the homes that encircle the island. It is amazing that people actually lived in the small dwellings seemingly chiseled into the rock, with only a few feet in front of the immense drop to the rocky ground below. I am certain many children died as results of falls from their homes above. Remember that the steps down to the bridge is a two-way walk. Climbing back up is not easy. Be sure to take a cold bottle of water with you as you tour this area.

The second most visited and photographed place in Arizona, next to the Grand Canyon, is Montezuma's Castle national monument, located 289 miles north of the junction of highways 10 and 17 in Phoenix. The beautiful cave apartment dwelling built into the high walls of the cliffs above is worth every mile and time you spend getting there. The front wall is made of stone with red rock mortar covering the entire length. The lazily flowing water of Beaver Creek just a hundred yards in front of the cliff home, with the canals leading to the fields of corn and squash across the water, offered the residents of this protected home everything they needed.

There is no entry allowed to the inside of the ruins, but there is an electronic audio presentation which explains the interior rooms of the dwelling above, and how they were used by the inhabitants. It is the highlight of the trip to be able to see the figures inside the rooms and hear how they worked and what they did up there those many hundreds of years ago. Why they left is a mystery to many visitors who flock there, after or before stopping at the Cliff Castle casino, on the same road just a few miles before entering the national monument.

If by chance you take the shortcut from Holbrook, Arizona, bypassing Flagstaff, down to Phoenix, there is a very interesting place to visit called the Tonto National Monument, four miles east of the Roosevelt Dam on highway 188. This is an accessible, beautiful cliff dwelling occupied by the Salado people during the 1100 to 1250 AD timeframe.

There are actually two cliff dwellings up in the cliffs above Lake Roosevelt, which offer a gorgeous view of the manmade lake which had been part of the Salt River system when these places were occupied by the Salado people. The lower ruins have a paved path leading up to them, but it is an uphill hike, more than a stroll. About half-way up, turn around and look out at the lake. If there are sailboats out that day it is a sight to behold. Leaving that location turn east on highway 188 going toward Globe, Arizona, which is a much easier and safer way to get into the valley and to Phoenix.

Globe, Arizona has its own Native American village called Besh ba Gowah, meaning "place of metal", which is a very easy "walk through" museum with a wonderful exhibit of adobe buildings and many items that have been found in the various archaeological digs in the four corners region. It is located on the far southern part of the city.

Another popular place to visit for tourists is the Casa Grande ruins in Coolidge, Arizona. The easy walk around the huge building and grounds offer one the opportunity of seeing the construction and engineering abilities these prehistoric people put to use. The logs that support the upper stories were from trees from as far away as 25 miles, and had to be transported from there to this place of the building.

The material used to construct the buildings was wetted clay found just below the desert surface, called caliche mud. The walls were hand-shaped, with each height and thickness approximately 24 inches tall and 30 inches thick at the bottom and gradually lessening the thickness as the height increased. Starting at the southeastern corner, after digging a deep trench around the entire base, they began forming the walls traveling from there to the northeast corner and around the entire structure. As they got to the starting point, they began the next row up as the first row had dried by that time.

The heavy wooden posts were inserted onto the walls and then covered over with the caliche mud hardening around the post as the builders moved on. Holes were left open at specific places to allow the person inside to catch the rays of sunshine on the solstice and other important dates of the year.

As the huge building rose in height, the master, or chief, living inside, oversaw the roof being applied. This was a building that has stood the test of time, having been built in the 1100's and standing until now in the 21st century. The route to the Casa Grande ruins is well marked along highway 10 south of Phoenix. The walls of the smaller buildings and the ball court are worth seeing, and the on-site rangers are very good at explaining the lives of these Hohokam people. Hohokam stands for "people who have gone before."

If you decide to stay within the Valley of the Sun, then while you are here there is a city park dedicated to the pueblo people who lived in a village next to the Salt River. Surprisingly, it is right next to the Phoenix Sky Harbor airport, and can be entered near the corner of 48th Street and Washington Street. It is called Pueblo Grande museum and contains many remains of the homes that were occupied by the pueblo people in the 1100's to about 1250 AD.

Another "don't miss" in the Phoenix area is the Heard Museum located at 22 East Monte Vista Road in Phoenix. This museum has collected and displays one of the most complete pueblo and indigenous guides into the lives of those people of long ago, as well as introducing us all to the descendants and the products they make now.

The Superstition Mountain museum on the Apache Trail, a few miles north of Apache Junction in the far East Valley, is another great peek into the lives and pages of history. Some of the interesting things to see and do there are to ride the old train they have there, see how they used the huge press to crush rock while searching for gold, watch the blacksmith grab hot metal from the bellows, bending it into horseshoes and other items the people of long ago wanted or needed. The white chapel you see as you approach the entryway to the museum is known as the Elvis Presley chapel, which was rescued along with the blacksmith shop from the devastating fire that destroyed the Apacheland movie studio in which many western movies were filmed in the 1950's.

A visitors' center is stocked with many items, books, edibles, jewelry, and also many interesting exhibits within the museum. A few hundred yards up the highway (88) is the reconstructed remains of an old ghost town called Goldfield. It was the source, at one time, of gold found by gold miners during the early 1900's. It is a fun place to visit as you can go underground in a mineshaft, see the shops as they appeared back in those early days, and get a bite to eat or a soft or hard drink at the saloon at the top of the hill.

Over that hill there is a horseback riding area so that those who want to say they rode in the Superstition Mountains can accomplish that. There is also an old jail house with bars you might duck behind while your family takes a picture of you in the hoosegow. It is a peek into the past that makes you realize people had lives that were of importance and interest to them, and a pathway that led their lives toward our own.

If you continue down Highway 10 to the east, there is another place that is worthwhile stopping at just north of Silver City, New Mexico called the Gila (Hela) Cliff Dwellings. It was one of the

122

villages that I talked about in my second and third books, "Shadows through a Spirit Window" and "Whispering Winds Remember." It takes a while to get there, but it is an interesting place to tour.

There are many, many more wonderful places and things to see regarding the prehistoric people who lived in the southwest, and I encourage readers to take advantage of a peek into the past, and visit these great historic places. Let your mind take you back to the time these places were teeming with people, just like you and me, playing and working through lives that have now been forgotten, except for these few moments when you can imagine their being there with you.

I hope that you have enjoyed and learned a few things about the lives of those people who lived many years ago in a very different way than we do, acquainted yourselves with the beautiful areas of North America, and have acquired an understanding of how far we have come from where they were to where we are now.

—Donald L Ensenbach, author.

www.ingramcontent.com/pod-product-compliance
Lightning Source LLC
Chambersburg PA
CBHW031535040426

42445CB00010B/550